Olof G. Lidin

Balance and Chance

BUNKA WENHUA

Tübinger Ostasiatische Forschungen
Tuebingen East Asian Studies

herausgegeben von/edited by

Klaus Antoni, Viktoria Eschbach-Szabo,
Robert Horres, Achim Mittag,
Gunter Schubert, Hans Ulrich Vogel

Band/Volume 18

LIT

Olof G. Lidin

Balance and Chance

The True Life

LIT

Published with the financial assistance of the Carlsberg Foundation (Copenhagen).

The transliteration used in this book is the traditional Wade-Giles system for Chinese and the Hepburn system for Japanese.

∞

Gedruckt auf alterungsbeständigem Werkdruckpapier entsprechend
ANSI Z3948 DIN ISO 9706

Bibliographic information published by the Deutsche Nationalbibliothek
The Deutsche Nationalbibliothek lists this publication in the Deutsche Nationalbibliografie; detailed bibliographic data are available in the Internet at http://dnb.d-nb.de.

ISBN 978-3-8258-1902-6

A catalogue record for this book is available from the British Library

Fresnostr. 2 D-48159 Münster
Tel. +49 (0) 2 51-620 32 22 Fax +49 (0) 2 51-922 60 99
e-Mail: lit@lit-verlag.de http://www.lit-verlag.de

Distribution:
In Germany: LIT Verlag Fresnostr. 2, D-48159 Münster
Tel. +49 (0) 2 51-620 32 22, Fax +49 (0) 2 51-922 60 99, e-Mail: vertrieb@lit-verlag.de

In Austria: Medienlogistik Pichler-ÖBZ GmbH & Co KG
IZ-NÖ, Süd, Straße 1, Objekt 34, A-2355 Wiener Neudorf
Tel. +43 (0) 22 36-63 53 52 90, Fax +43 (0) 22 36-63 53 52 43, e-Mail: mlo@medien-logistik.at

In Switzerland: B + M Buch- und Medienvertriebs AG
Hochstr. 357, CH-8200 Schaffhausen
Tel. +41 (0) 52-643 54 85, Fax +41 (0) 52-643 54 35, e-Mail: order@buch-medien.ch

Distributed in the UK by: Global Book Marketing, 99B Wallis Rd, London, E9 5LN
Phone: +44 (0) 20 8533 5800 – Fax: +44 (0) 1600 775 663
http://www.centralbooks.co.uk/html

Distributed in North America by:

Transaction Publishers
New Brunswick (U.S.A.) and London (U.K.)

Transaction Publishers
Rutgers University
35 Berrue Circle
Piscataway, NJ 08854

Phone: +1 (732) 445 - 2280
Fax: + 1 (732) 445 - 3138
for orders (U. S. only):
toll free (888) 999 - 6778
e-mail: orders@transactionpub.com

Contents

Introduction

It is said that "A big book is a big evil" (G. E. Lessing, 1729-1781). And that "what is said simply is heard." The 125 brief chapters contain one message: how to find the inner-outer Balance and lead the fulfilled and happy life. They are based on personal experiences over a long life. The approach is as eastern as it is western, and references are made equally East and West. The discourse is not academic, but in an easy-to-read form – without heavy, convoluted psycho-speak. About half a century ago it dawned on the writer that all life, not least human life, is an inner-outer mélange under the Eternal and Balance and Chance. One can be suspicious of intuitive life, but when it has worked over a fifty-year period, one becomes convinced that there is a world more real than the terrestrial world, that it directs and leads and that its Will can be trusted. The intuitive experience becomes the guidance.

The vision of a timeless and changeless logic that surpasses human knowledge breeds joy and happiness. Critics are apt to call this intuitive life escapism, self-deception and wishful thinking. They consider that the unseen order should not be trusted. It is the writer's conviction, however, that we can trust our intuitive life and allow daily life to be led by it. If we seek truth inwards and trust intuition, we will live the rich life we are born for.

The goal of spiritual endeavour throughout the ages has been the full and happy life. A wealth of literature over the ages bears witness to this. The sources are innumerable and it seems somewhat overbearing to produce another work on the subject. Only a new approach and a life's experience can vindicate the project. Today's thinkers have in common that they both begin and end in this world. They are few who begin and end on the other side. For a happy life you need to seek Balance first in the inner and then allow Chance to work in the outer.

Part I: Oneness

1. Look up, feel in and be happy!

What does one see all around? Balance and Chance. Nature is full of it. Everyone is full of it. Looking up into the network of branches of a tree, one sees how Chance has created a design in Balance. When one looks within, one senses the presence of a force striving for Balance. There is a Will pulsing throughout the Whole[1], and it can be designated Chance, and throughout the Whole there is Meaning and Purpose. The sum of all things is the ever-shifting Balance. Together they form the Cosmic Order. The Eternal[2] directs Chance and shapes Balance in the grand cosmic evolution. Hence, Balance and Chance are the two modes of being and becoming.[3]

Just as a coin needs its flipside, the Temporal cannot do without the Eternal and the Eternal cannot do without the Temporal. The natural reality is the "stuff." It requires the precious spark of Chance to acquire the form of a man, a woman or any other object. Living in the world of sensory perception, one touches the manifold forms into which it has transformed. One sees and hears, smells and tastes – and feels.[4] The senses are directed outwards, and one therefore comprehends the equilibrium of things. One sees a tree and hears a song, one smells a cheese and tastes a cake. One feels more, however, when the senses are still. One feels whether soul and body are in or out of Balance. One feels the unity, the Balance and the Grand Oneness of the Whole.[5]

---

1 The Whole has been defined as the "Unity of all reality."

2 The yonder transcendent Being, the nameless *Tao*, God, Gods, Godheads in religions, the Evolution, the *fons et origo* of all Becoming and Plato's World Soul. The Eternal Will compares with *tendô*, "Heaven's Way", in Chinese thought. Compare with Marcus Aurelius' Inner Cause.

3 *Tao-Te-Ching* says that it is a natural process: "everything becoming so of itself." Balance is found on every level of Creation, Chance being its handmaiden. Hu Shih 1934, p. 81.

4 Feeling in its widest sense, including emotion and sentiment.

5 R. L. Taylor 1988, p. 14, and H. D. Thoreau 1949, p. 212. Why do we always have to understand and to know? As Picasso says, "Why do you not try to understand the songs of birds?"

As Marcus Aurelius says, "Look within; within is the fountain of all good."

2. Feeling rather than Reason

Man's soul is a double mirror that reflects both inwards and outwards. Where the senses stop, feeling takes over and reach farther. Feeling has a broader scope, speaks a richer language and exists at a deeper, more unfathomable level, removing the curtain that separates being from appearance, rational from irrational.

The mind is thus Janus-faced and registers both what comes from the inner and what comes from the outer, what the intellect perceives and the heart learns. What cannot be known, can be felt. Emotions determine the quality of our lives and concern all human dispositions. They are both positive and negative, and need be cultivated and tended. "The emotional nature is the essence of human nature," says the Chinese philosopher Hsün Tzu.[6]

Immanuel Kant (1724-1804) pointed out that the faculty of reasoning is limited.[7] This might come as a surprise in a world where reason is affirmed priority over feeling. Reason has, however, a value of its own. It is indispensable in man's earthly life. It makes him the human person that differs from other living creatures. It makes him develop tools and laws. Mathematics serves as his handmaiden when things are observed and measured scientifically and mechanically.

In spite of recent efforts in neuroscience the mathematics of feeling has not yet been developed.[8] It trails behind more objective science, dis-

---

6 L. L. Whyte (1896-1972) similarly, "The springs of human nature lie in the unconscious, for it links the individual with the universal ... whether it is expressed as the union of the soul with the divine, or as the realm which links the moments of human awareness with the background of organic processes within which they emerge." In his *The Unconscious before Freud*, p. 70.

7 Today's science agrees with Kant. "Heisenberg in physics and Godel in mathematics have shown ineluctable limits to human reason." W. Barrett 1956, pp. x-xi.

8 For an analysis of feeling, emotion and sentiment see A. R. Damasio 2003, pp. 3-179. Compare D. Lack 1961, p. 114: "Science has not accounted for morality, truth, beauty, individual responsibility and self-awareness ... in which case a valid and central part of human experience lies outside science [and reason]." As

regarded and ignored by all those who devote their undivided attention to reason. However, man cannot live by reason alone.[9] To use reason to understand "the limitless room within" is, as Karen Armstrong puts it, "as meaningless as to eat soup with a fork."[10] How can one possibly measure love, lust and passion?

We should note the imbalance when one side of human nature predominates at the expense of the other which should be accorded equal weight and consideration. Man must live with feeling as much as with reason provided he desires a happy life. Equipped with the tool of reason, he can build much, however armed with feeling, he is capable of building more and living happier. It is the tragedy of modern man that as a cognitive being he tends to forget that true life includes – and begins with – affective and intuitive perception. It should be as much, "I feel, therefore I am" (*sentio, ergo sum*) as "I think, therefore I am." (*cogito, ergo sum*).[11]

Only the proper mix of feeling and reason will ultimately enable him to lead the fulfilled life. Both intermingled results in the whole person, only one of the two in a stunted personality,[12]

Henry David Thoreau (1817-1862) recommends man to "Feel inner – and go forth!"

3. Reason and Feeling in Harmony

Ultimately, Feeling colours the totality of being and encompasses all things and circumstances. It covers the entire range from Temporality to Eternity. It joins with divine Truth and Purpose and moves into the world of temporal finiteness. All religion, ethics and aesthetics are rooted in it.

---

there are feelings inspired by outer emotions there are feelings emanated from inner life. Outer feelings are "largely constituted by the perception of ... body states" (A. R. Damasio 2003, p. 89) while inner feelings "lie in harmoniously ... adjusting to an unseen order" (W. James 1963, p. 53).

9 T. Sorell 2005, p. x.

10 K. Armstrong 2005a, p. 104.

11 "Feeling is everything", says Faust, "Order is everything", says Adrian, "Pure feeling is the source and the essence of religion," says W. R. Inge 1925.

12 Jean-Jacques Rousseau (1712-1778) puts feeling over reason and stresses its superiority over the intellect. See *La nouvelle Héloise*, his novel from 1761, and Will and Ariel Durant 1967, pp. 165-170.

One is capable of feeling whether awake or asleep. It has been said that everyone belongs to an Indra's net of sentiment and that everything which is not speakable thought, is the faculty of feeling. Calming the finite mind and looking inward, one becomes aware that life includes an infinite reality of pure being, which transcends forms and names.[13]

By means of feeling one removes barriers and finds rapport with the Whole which is more than the sum of its animate and inanimate constituents. Man can feel his way *à l'infini*. He can not reason his way there. Feeling moves from heart to heart,[14] it pervades reality and attains the soul where all is all and all sings all. If the entryways of perception and thought are cleansed, everything will appear to man as it is, infinite and divine.

Reason can never match feeling in range or depth. It can help open the window to Eternity, but cannot enter it. It does not cover the entire picture, but allied with the limitless feeling it begets the complete man. "Though essential to understanding, it does not control thought and behaviour."[15] "We do not fall in love, or enjoy music, or lick our lips over strawberries, for *reasons*. The end of our behaviour is set by our desires, our tastes – our *feeling* patterns."[16]

4. *Mens sana in corpore sano*

The Romans spoke of "a healthy mind in a healthy body" (*mens sana in corpore sano*). They understood that man's mental processes are just as

---

[13] For a comparison, feeling is the software which provides instructions to the hardware, that is, the senses. Today the emphasis is on the hardware. The software is as necessary as the hardware, just as form (Chin. *li*, Jap. *ri*) is as important as matter (Chin. *ch'i*, Jap. *ki*) in Chinese philosophy. When scholars today find conscious life "mysterious" it might be because they treat it as just a "cognitive phenomenon" and forget its inner emotive half. (L. Wittgenstein, 1889-1951).

[14] The Japanese use the term *ishin-denshin*, "communication heart with heart" for non-sensory telepathic communion.

[15] L. L. Whyte 1979, p. 49 and pp. 99-100. G. W. Leibniz (1646-1716) says, "Our clear concepts are like islands which arise above the ocean."

[16] B. Magee 1998, pp. 115-116. For emotions, see P. Ekman 2003, a work that begins with the statement, "Emotions determine the quality of our lives. They occur in every relationship."

important as his physical reality. Together, in harmony and unity, they form the complete person who is able to take on the problems of the world and fulfil his allotted task.

This sense of proportion has been lost with the focus on all sorts of artificialities which have come to dominate life. As long as man's efforts were merely directed at having what was necessary, this was not serious. Now, however, the situation has changed. Man has created contrivances in abundance, far more plentiful than he could have dreamed of in former times. Settling down amongst them and allowing them to control life, the situation has become alarming.

Each human person is born into a life shaped as much by sentiment as by reason. A full life craves a whole being, and a whole being, in turn, craves balance and equanimity. It should come as no surprise that man's body needs to be fit, but, equally, that man's inner also needs to be in trim. Much effort is made today for physical health whereas mental health is more often than not neglected. Inner fitness should, however, be is natural as outer fitness. In the saying "mens sana" comes first while "corpore sano" comes second.

5. Inner Life and Outer Life

The interior world of the soul is as complex as the exterior physical world. It has its own geography, its mountains and valleys. Nobody can fathom its depth. The eyes are directed towards the outside world, and it need not be quibbled about the fact that man was designed and born to live in this ever-changing world. He was created to deal with a reality in which survival was precarious, where life was up against enormous odds. From the perspective of countless millennia, it is a miracle that mankind survived at all. Nonetheless, it is also clear that man maintained a sense of proportion throughout the ages. He was never totally absorbed by the physical reality. The invisible was always as real to him as the visible. Essence paired existence.[17]

---

[17] "The visible world is part of a more spiritual universe from which it draws its chief significance, and that harmonious relation with that higher universe is our true end." (W. James 1963)

Modern anthropological studies of early cultures unravel the same picture everywhere. Natural phenomena were always coupled with an immaterial world. The reality embraced the beyond that, always, in one way or another, interfered with matters in the tangible world.[18] The beyond joined the here and now inescapably and played a role in human life. It was a natural part of daily life and nothing was undertaken without being preceded with ceremonies, rites and offerings.

It can, of course, be asserted that it was the lack of knowledge and the uncertainty of the early ages that paved the way for their 'naïve' beliefs. But just imagine the perseverance and ubiquity of the so-called primitive thought! There was no people around the globe that did not see things along the same numinous lines. History attests to how inspiration led to great deeds and triumphs in science, literature and, really, in all fields. "The European culture is the result of Christianity."[19] The inner light was needed for anything of worth to be accomplished. The intellectualism of our latter day robs mankind of the balanced and harmonious outlook on life that was the source of creativity in days gone by.

6. Redressing the Balance *pari passu*

An upset balance can be redressed. This is neither impossible nor infeasible. While this balancing may seem afar in a world out of equilibrium, it need not be. It can actually be achieved easily, if one is prepared to make the effort. And there are as many paths leading us to this goal as there are people on earth. Common for all of them, however, is the requirement that the individual goes within.[20] He must, as it were, turn his eyes around. He must allow them to gaze inwards and touch the wide vistas where calm and nonattachment reign and the mind is at rest. As Lao Tzu said, "To the mind that is still, the whole universe surrenders," and Chuang Tzu[21] adds, "and sees all in one." Only in the recesses of the soul, where feeling and reason proceed *pari passu*, the harmony of the

---

[18] For primitive man "all is religion; he perpetually lives in a world of mysticism and ritualism." B. Malinowski 1948, p. 24.

[19] This is the view of Pope Benedict XVI.

[20] All we seek is already within ourselves," says S. Einhorn 1998, p. 166.

[21] *Lao Tzu*, ch. 35, and *Chuang Tzu*, ch. 22.

pervading Whole and the luminous quality of the mind are experienced. Throughout runs a sentiment of unity and beauty, as shining, clear and distinct on the inside as on the outside. As a result of this equipoise, one is happy and finds the entire universe a delight. "A man should learn to detect and watch that gleam of light which flashes across his mind from within."[22]

Henry David Thoreau says in his *Walden*,

> Direct your eyes right inward, and you'll find
> A thousand regions in your mind,
> Yet undiscovered ...[23]

In the words of William Blake (1757-1827),

> Inwards, inwards, inwards,
> To the eternal worlds!

This act of redressing the Balance need not be anything remarkable: To let the mind and spirit come to rest, one can just sit and enjoy being, clearing the mind, turning the heart in, and allowing the intuitive voice to attune. What one has to learn is to penetrate to the interior! It might take time to train the eyes not just to look but to see. It can be a few minutes at a time and be part of other activities. If one realises first the treasure within, then the outside world will become rich too.[24] True Balance requires as much looking inwards as outwards.

If what is within is in harmony and order, life runs like a poem, becomes a journey of happiness and one finds that this is a world of plenty. All people have, at one time or another, gained nourishment from the "flash from the fountain of the heart" (Jacob Böhme), without realising that it is the height of living. Is it not true that people miss their great moments because they take them for granted at the time they live them and forget them?[25]

---

[22] Ralph Waldo Emerson (1803-1882), quoted in T. V. Smith and E. C. Lindeman 1951, p. 89. Emerson's transcendental thought is generally close to what is expressed in this work. See, for example, R. L. Rusk 1949, in toto.

[23] Thoreau 1949, p. 213.

[24] As Buddha expressed it, "Buddhahood is *within* you, the law is within you and *salvation* is within you." Hu Shih 1934, pp. 86-87.

[25] Jacob Böhme (1575-1624) has expressed the same in *Vom übersinnlichen Leben: "Es ist in dir, und so du magst eine Stunde schweigen von allem deinem Wollen und Sinnes: so wirst du unaussprechliche Worte GOTTES hören – Wenn du von*

In *Zen* meditation it is demanded that one sits erect, breathes calmly in and out and even watches one's breath. This is the way for the few who can spend years at a temple. For the many the seeking of the intuitive truth must be simple. It is wonderful to read the words of Tenzin Palmo, an English nun, "You can meditate walking down the corridor, waiting for the traffic lights to change, at the computer, standing in a queue, in the bathroom, combing your hair. Just be there in the present, without the mental commentary."[26] Meditation should be a normal life just "looking into oneself." The Japanese Buddhist Shinran (1173-1263)[27] recommends: "always with [the *mantra*][28] *Namu Amida Buddha* ("Honour to the Amida Buddha") in your mind and on your lips![29]

7. People Differ and the Routes Are Many

There are as many routes as there are individual souls. The manifold paths of religion have been trodden by believers throughout history. Many experience the moment of sublimity in temples, churches, mosques or other holy houses. They are not necessarily clergy and men of holy orders, caught in the rituals and ceremonies of institutional religion. Many more are the little people and believers who come for solace and comfort. We perceive more often than not more sincerity in the back pews of a church or on the uppermost gallery of a theatre than in the front rows.

Sinnen und Wollen deiner Selbheit stille stehest, so wird in dir das ewige Hören, Sehen, und Sprechen offenbar und höret und siehet GOTT durch dich. Dein eigen Hören, Wollen und Sehen verhindert dich, dass du Gott nicht siehest und hörest." (It is in you, and you must for a while still all your desires and senses: and you will hear the inexpressible GOD's words – When you remain still, the Eternal hearing, seeing and speaking will be apparent and you hear and see GOD through you. Your own hearing, desiring and seeing hinders you from seeing and hearing God.) See L. Schreyer 1920, p. 333.

26 Tenzin Palmo is quoted in M. Ricard 2006, p. 230. She is close to Shinran in Japan who preaches constant reciting of the Amida *mantra*.

27 Shinran was the founder of Japan's largest Buddhist sect, the *Jôdo shinshû*, characterised by its faith in Amida Buddha.

28 *Mantra* is a prayer-like utterance, recited or sung, first of all in Hinduism and Buddhism. Much prayer is like *mantra*.

29 Gautama Buddha's injunction, "Look within, ... be a lamp into yourself!"

In this age of scepticism, with its disregard for religion and over-sensitivity toward anything that smacks of religious myth, it is time to venture into new avenues. Unity can be brought back to a seemingly split world. People should act individually, leaving behind the domes and cathedrals where religion is entrapped, congealed and hardened.[30] Anything that can be achieved in a congregation or a group can also be achieved in solitude. Man is capable of establishing his own holy place in private life. He is capable of attaining his own Balance where his senses transcend time and space on the boundary between thought and sentiment.

People differ. Each has his unique qualities. While one person may need complete solitude to accomplish his serenity, another may require a lively café. While one person best achieves his harmony with one foot on the accelerator, speeding down a highway, another might enjoy inner peace with a pipe in hand, or better, refreshed by music, even with the television on, whereas yet others may achieve their happiness caught in the motions of a dance around a totem pole or in contemplation of a Buddha image. While one person can best do it in the early morning, another while lost in the depths of sleep and dream at night. Some are too drowsy in the morning while others are too tired in the evening. Some may find that a combination of sensations around them will help them to new and fresh experience. One way or another, however, a person must be on his own, for the most part in silence and doing little more than contemplating – looking inward and upward.[31]

A. North Whitehead (1861-1947) wrote that "if you are never solitary, you are never religious," implying that solitude and quietude are the finest music in striving for your mind's calm and harmony. Generally speaking, it is advisable to avoid standardised procedures, so popular with clerics. Rituals may have suited the lifestyle of the devout in the past; in this secularised epoch, however, such standardised acts are best avoided. It is up to the individual to reach within in his quest for the intuitive truth. It might require some effort but it will lead to a sense of ful-

---

30 "In the end religions are symbolic of what is higher" (Viscount Haldane 1929, p. 348) and must stretch to the experiences of inner psychic life in relation to an unseen order that is considered divine.

31 "Contentment enhances our enjoyment and diminishes our misery." F. J. Sheen 1951, p. 9.

filment and happiness that will last until his last day. It is worth remembering Dostoevsky's words that "we are all happy if we but knew it."

8. The Good Mood

Rocking chair, pipe, background music, these are all but auxiliary means creating and setting the mood. A good mood assists all relations. Who does not like to see a happy face? And who does not like to be happy with himself? It is easy to understand people who take to the bottle. Do not problems always look better from the bottom of a glass! At least for a short while? Eating and drinking well, a good cigar, a smile, a friendly nod or word, doesn't it all help to evoke the good mood? When we talk about "good service", we generally express satisfaction with our place of sitting, whether in a restaurant, a taxi or any other place. A good mood ought not to be scorned or disregarded; after all, it is the stepping-stone to great joy.

Once we are in good spirit, we are already removed from the dreariness of reality, which has the potential to destroy any mood. To be able to handle any situation, it helps being a couple of steps removed and seeing things from a distance. The detachment that comes hand in hand with a good disposition, makes it easier to look through and tackle a problem. How often does it not happen that a smile emanating from good spirits creates the bridge across, facilitating contact and bringing two people closer to an understanding? And how often does not a dash of good humour springing from a cheerful face, melt the ice between strangers and defrost a conversation?

In our rational world it might seem that the rational mood is preferred. The electronic frame of mind has invaded our modern world, with the computer being its most evident component. Doing without dream, vision and fantasy, man attempts to solve all problems in a square, digital manner and tends to equate economic prosperity with happiness.[32] He has the globe in his hands – but not his subtle inner. The result is a one-dimensional reality, in which his soul remains starved and forsaken.

---

[32] See G. H. von Wright 1963, p. 95 *et passim.*

9. Peace of Mind

Turning the gaze inwards is not so complicated as it might seem. Leaning back in the armchair, looking within, relaxing, day-dreaming, one can arrive at one's heart's stillness. It is where the timeless fragrance of eternity and fleeting temporality meet.[33] At this juncture one evokes harmony and encounters one's peace of mind. There in the midst of a sea of feeling a person is at his fullest. He is free, he fathoms the Whole, that carries all reality in its stream, and he is one with everything. It is at once both feeling and consciousness. Duality is transcended. One gives oneself to the moment when divine inspiration plays by whim, when roads open up, when "the cup runneth full" and "you pierce through a glass beyond which you now see darkly."[34] It is pure bliss. One sees what is to be done or left undone and what route to take.[35]

When serenity is thus complete, harmonies appear wherever eyes look. Inner music creates outer music, and inner beauty generates outer beauty. One does not need to go in search of the fountain of the Eternal and infinite truth; it cascades there where one sits and stands. When a person is aware of and responds to the spirit within, Chance serves him in unforeseeable ways and opportunities present themselves. Uncertainty is gone and joy fills body and soul.[36]

In this instance of immediate experience heavens open. It is "intuition of pure Will, free of the troubles and perplexities and confusions of intellect – how happy, how free." It cannot be manifested by the usual five senses, such as sight and sound, but by another sense that may be described as pure Feeling or Being. It can be taken religiously when one feels the Eternal in every minute and every speck of space. Walt Whit-

---

[33] The dictum *Know thyself* and the admonition to *look within* is found in all religions and philosophies. "One must first know one's soul before he can know his Lord," says Ibn Arabi (1165-1240). See J. C. Cooper 1981, pp. 86-89.

[34] Free rendering of 1st Epistle of Paul to the *Corinthians*, 13: 11.

[35] From Lao Tzu in the sixth century B.C. who expressed the "feeling of empathy with other things." Today T'ang Chün-i describes how "this relation of mutual empathy is shared by the conscious self even with animals and purely material objects like stones." T. A. Metzger 1977, p. 35.

[36] J. C. Eccles 1980, pp. 245-246.

man (1819-1892) expressed this when he acclaimed the wonder of nature in the *Leaves of Grass*. All was 'peace and joy' around him.[37]

Henri Bergson (1859-1941) says that "we live simultaneously in two worlds, the inner world of *élan vital* ('vital impulse') and the outer world presented to us by our intellect. We live in a perpetual stream of forces and our lives are illuminated in their midst," that "We must pass from static outer religion to dynamic inner religion" and that "impetus comes from inspiration and intuition, not from reason and intelligence."[38]

10. The Inner Direction

Balance is nothing static and changeless, it has many forms and appearances. Nor is man unchanging. World-views differ from individual to individual and from situation to situation. What is certain is that each individual possesses his psychic world, just as his physical world, and secondly that there is travel between the two worlds. These have to be in proportion to one another for a peaceful and happy life, with the vast interior world given priority. People differ and it is up to each person to hit upon his own mode to coordinate his mind and spirit. Intuition is a talent that can be developed and some concentration may be required but a willingness amply suffices to open the door to one's inner self – and let the inner speak. Exertion is required to let go of wayward anxieties and to remain relaxed and calm, and in stillness attain the liberty of authentic existence and allow intuitive clarity to be the beacon of life.

Man mostly dwells in the range of his psyche set aside for reasoning. In order to move to where thinking and non-thinking converge, he must 'inscend' from mind to heart. This should constitute the initial stage, only as long as it takes to proceed through the confines of conscious-

---

[37] As J. Horgan says, "Minds without emotions are not really minds at all. They are souls on ice – cold lifeless creatures devoid of any desires, ... pains or pleasures." J. Horgan 1999, p. 29.

[38] B. Magee 1998, p. 215, and E. Cassirer 1944, pp. 102-103f. See H. Bergson 1933, pp. 175f., and H. Bergson 1929b, p. 89 and p. 91. W. James (1842-1910) says that "Religion is the rational by-product, a 'crystallisation', of inner experience." In W. James 1963.

ness,[39] that is, "from outer awareness to inner awareness where the wonder is felt."[40] Arthur Koestler (1905-1983) says, "The springs of human nature lie in the unconscious."[41]

It is your duty, says Jakob Böhme, "to press into the centre, ... be silent before the Lord, sitting alone with him in your inmost and most hidden cell, your inward being centrally united in itself." Robert Browning (1812-1889) says that "There is an inmost centre in us all, where truth abides in fullness ..." He continues: "God is seen in the star, in the stone, in the flesh, in the soul and the clod." The Eternal has its Will which, in Jacob Böhme's words, "seeks itself and finds itself in itself ... and is the flowing out of the divine Wisdom."[42] And Plotinus says that for the immediate apprehension of the divine truth we only need "the faculty which all possess, but few use."[43]

11. The Point of Balance and the Centre of the Heart

The Point of Balance is located on the border of the limitless ocean of infinity. Where the world of reason and the depths of feeling intersect is the point.[44] In a manner of speaking, an axis runs through the psyche and this very point on the axis is where introspection should be directed. This

---

[39] Consciousness is understood as "every kind of psychism, from the most rudimentary forms of interior perception imaginable to the human phenomenon of reflective thought." T. de Chardin 1955, p. 57. "Consciousness is beyond the reach of human intelligence", according to Antonio Damasio. It stands for a person's "I" and "me" in common life and parlance.

[40] J. Gaarder 1991, p. 369. "A mystery is that which excites curiosity, surmise or wonder, yet baffles our attempt to explain it" (Webster's Dictionary).

[41] L. L. Whyte 1979, Introduction by Arthur Koestler. Koestler clarifies the unconscious as "the realm which links the moments of human awareness with the background of organic processes within which they emerge." Further, W. R. Inge (1860-1954) says, "Since the attempt to explain the mind materialistically and life mechanically appears to have failed, nothing remains to but to explain nature spiritually." W. R. Inge 1925, p. 371.

[42] J. Böhme is quoted in F. C. Happold 1963, p. 72, R. Browning on p. 60 and p. 92.

[43] Plotinus quoted in A. Fox 1960, p. 158. Sigmund Freud (1856-1939) says that happiness "by its very nature cannot be more than an episodic phenomenon."

[44] Chuang Tzu says, "This point is the motionless centre on the rim of which all contingencies, distinctions and individualities resolve; and from it only Infinity is to be seen, which is neither this nor that, nor yes nor no. To see all in the yet

can be done on the knees, it can be done 'on the couch', and it can be done in one's premises or in the silence of a dome. One can do it with eyes open, or with eyes closed. Sitting, standing, moving, the same awareness is recognised. Allowing one's inner to be in stillness, it can be done at any time and only requires the gazing inwards. One's 'vagabond mind' (Descartes) must stop wandering and the senses be checked and restrained.

Once one arrives at this inner centre of consciousness between outer intellect and inner feeling, one need not go farther. The introspection should not plunge deeper into the ocean of feeling,[45] as this is not Balance. A sense of overflowing joy is the corroborating evidence that one has attained 'the Kingdom of Heaven.' Privately one needs no more proof, but in case others are sceptical – as doubting Thomases tend to be – one's personal sincerity should be proof enough.

The first time one senses the overpowering sensation of Balance one will know the meaning of happiness. It is the supreme pleasure that one wants to hold on to for ever. Unfortunately, it is not a sensation that endures after it has been experienced. The world sees to it that, more often than not, one loses touch with the inner vision. The everyday life, situational experiences, material worry and misery, social relations, all serve to disturb the joyful bliss.[46]

The Balance may therefore be transient, since the external environment is in constant change. The equilibrium is often not guided from the inside but from the outside. One reads more about and hears more often of the "other-directed" man than the "inner-directed" man. This is ines-

---

indifferentiated primordial unity, or from such a distance that all melts into one, this is true intelligence." Translation in J. C. Cooper 1981, p. 27.

45 C. G. Jung (1875-1961) would perhaps more learnedly talk about "a transcendent directive centre of the psyche in the self." M. Nagy 1991, p. 46.

46 This experience is described by Hildegard of Bingen (1098-1179): "Since my childhood I have always seen a light in my soul, but not with the outer eyes, nor through the thoughts of my heart; neither do the five outer senses take part in this vision. ... This is much brighter than the cloud which bears the sun. ... What I see and learn in such a vision stays on in my memory. I see, hear and know in the same moment ... I sometimes see in it another light that is known to me as the living light. ... While I am enjoying the spectacle of this light, all sadness and sorrow vanish from my memory." Quotation in C. G. Jung and R. Wilhelm 1962, p. 106. Why deny one half of the psyche, the half that stretches via the heart into the inner and only trust the half that stretches via the intellect into the outer? The psychic balance requires both halves.

capable as the world takes over and the inner-directed individual is becoming a rare phenomenon. Jung deplores that "the cultivation of rational consciousness in the West has torn to shreds the belief of an earlier age" and that therefore "European man shows an alarming lack of balance."[47]

12. The Life of Minimum

Thus, external phenomena represent an obstacle for anyone wishing to fulfil his psychic life. Being focused on the exterior world and surrounded by all manner of things, it is not easy to maintain one's sang-froid. Consequently, it becomes necessary for a person to endeavour to limit attachment and expectation. What is recommended is the minimal life. It should be one's goal to acquire only the minimum of clothes, food and lodging, and also the minimum of other goods required for a normal life. The emphasis must be on what is necessary, and attachment to superficialities be avoided.[48]

Asceticism can be as wrong and mistaken as decadence and excess. Here too minimum is preferred.This can prove to be difficult in a world populated by worshippers of the pervasive materialism, demanding that more and more products be sold, all in the name of progress (and GNP).[49] And the glorification of the millionaire, nowadays even the billionaire! It is said that "rich people are poor people with money" and that "if you realize that you have enough, you are truly rich." Anyone striving to attain the felicity of Balance should keep his needs and desires to a minimum, but not less! One shall stave off the yearning for gold, and combat the greed for cash to the extent that these things are rendered superfluous. They should be recognised as little more than ash and dust and not be permitted to rule one's life. Truly, there is an affinity between scant material wealth and mental poise.[50] One thing matches the other.

---

47 C. G. Jung 1984, p. 266.

48 We should strive to be as minimal as nature.

49 Modern progress is nothing short of competitive economic growth. See Ch. Lasch 1991, p. 40 *et passim*.

50 Horace (65-8 B.C.), likewise, "warned that the race for public honours traps men, for the urge to glory and praise ruins both wellborn and lowly": 'Those who seek much, lack much'." D. Loy 2000, p. 135.

The ideal of being, unaffected by fame and fortune, has never been better expressed than by the Taoist philosopher Lao Tzu in China:

> The five colors
> blind our eyes.
> The five notes
> deafen our ears.
> The five flavours
> dull our taste
>
> Racing, chasing, hunting,
> drives people crazy.
> Trying to get rich
> ties people in knots.
>
> So the wise soul
> watches with the inner
> not the outward eye, letting that go,
> keeping this.[51]

The ideal is also well expressed by Confucius (551-479 B.C.) who says:

> How admirable Hui is! Living in a mean dwelling on a bowlful of rice and a ladleful of water is a hardship most men would find intolerable, but Hui does not allow this to affect his joy. How admirable Hui is![52]

13. Detached and Attached

We face the accusation that man, retreating into his mental tranquillity, is not engaged in the affairs of the world. It is even said that, once Balance has been achieved, a person comes to a standstill, his life stops and progress ends. This is said about India justifiably, and about China and Medieval Europe rather inaccurately. It is here a matter of the degree of the withdrawal. The Indian, retiring into his own fathomless self, stays there, forgetting the illusory world. The same cannot be said about philosophers in China, nor about the medieval monks in Europe. Confucian

---

51 *Lao Tzu*, ch. 12. Translation by Ursula K. Le Guin 1997, p. 15.

52 *Lun Yü* VI: 9. Translation by D. C. Lau 1983, p. 82. *Tao-te-ching* is translated as "The Classic of Tao and its Power" by Benjamin Schwartz. See also *the Analects* VII: 15 where Confucius says, "He who seeks only coarse food to eat, water to drink and bent arm for pillow, will without looking for it find happiness to boot." Translation by A. Waley 1938.

philosophers wished to play a role and function in society, and they did – whenever they were allowed. This was the ultimate goal of learning. Even the Taoist was never completely withdrawn from the world; in his own fashion, through alchemy, geomancy and other ventures, he made himself of use to humanity as he pursued longevity. Similarly the medieval monks were actively involved, building hospitals, tending the poor and needy, and serving as the salt of the earth. Both Chinese philosophers and European monks were vehicles of advancing civilizations. They were the intellectual backbone of society, East and West, without whom the lands would, truly, have been barbarous.

Neither Chinese philosophers nor medieval monks were in any doubt about the importance of the interior half of life. Efforts began there and only when self-realization was attained, was the philosopher or monk ready for participation in the world. Detached from the world, he could be truly engaged in it. "Only then can he set out and take on the turmoil and sickness of our time" (L. van der Post, 1906-1996).

As long as life's equilibrium is dominated by outer factors and the soul is ignored, there will be bias and prejudice in judgment and action. Society sees to it that the gaze is turned outward. The lives are full of distractions, irritations and problems to make even the most serene harmony tilt the concentration to the maze of the world. A knock on the door disrupts Faust's "visions at their fullest flower, his happiest, fairest hour." The threat lurks that Balance becomes world-determined and fixated on deceptive appearances to the extent that one judges life through the values of the world.

The man in Balance does not forsake the world. He does not live in a cage. His life is not asceticism for asceticism's sake. It might be an Indian ideal to withdraw and work on the salvation in solitary confinement. It is rather the responsibility of the individual who has managed his *felice-beato* to be active in the world. It is not the Buddha but the Bodhisattva who represents the ideal. Unattached, he is ready for attachment.

14. Materialism versus Inner Light

People should strive for the right proportions of mental life. The two halves of the psyche should be kept in a state of equilibrium, neither prevented from growing at the expense of the other. The unconscious part of the mind should serve the conscious part of the mind, and the conscious part the unconscious part. The inner in the outer and the outer in the inner must form a unity, and life should be lived at the intersection of the psyche where they meet. Only then people will have true life in their grasp, with depression and gloom banished, and happiness will be their lot even in times of adversity.

This can be difficult in a society that is increasingly depersonalised and materialised. Today mankind has become fixated on the exterior life whereas spiritual needs are discredited. Everything seems to be a mechanical, rational order. Where can Chance then come in and play a role? Man has erased the social slums only to build mental slums. In a computerised, digital society man's intuitive and immediate powers are lost. He has created a spiritless capitalism, he is trapped in it and shaped by it. The only eloquent reality is the concretely visible world. He bombards his psyche with events, facts and notions, which accumulate over time and years. He renovates his house and rooms in which he lives his physical life, but he avoids renovating his inner rooms – the fountain of life – which should come first! He allows new furniture to bring in its train sensory pleasures at the same time as his mental soul is neglected. Everyone has heard tales from tourists visiting poor lands expressing amazement at the warmth they meet among people who own little. On the other hand, a visitor from a poor land in a developed country blurts out: "People have forgotten to smile here!"

Truly, people are losing something in their materialised lives! Smiles and laughs are one thing, warmth and tenderness another. The question they should ask is how long the human climate can exist without either. To be honest, the machine is there, it has been built and it has many positive aspects. It cannot and should not be rejected. However, the present duty is to induce warmth and compassion, smiles and laughter into its structure. Simply, man must restore the psychic contents[53] of the machine before it overwhelms and destroys him. "He should bring Heaven down to earth and raise earth up to Heaven and himself be the happy

---

[53] For example, "images, sensations, thoughts, emotions", as proposed by M. Gundry 2006, p. 73.

mean."[54] When he ties his hopes and dreams only to the external world, he ends up being disappointed.

Unfortunately, traditional religion appears, often, to be outdated, and psychotherapy no more than placebo.[55] Freudian theories are popularly accepted but their efficacy as regards alleviation of mental disorder is limited.[56] Neither the priest nor the therapist should be disregarded but neither should the *personal happiness* achieved by turning the soul's eye toward the inner light.[57] With inner Balance, one is ready and equipped, like the Chinese philosopher and the medieval monk, for true social participation.

15. Inner Life First, Outer Life Second

It cannot be emphasised enough that outer life must be paired with the realisation of the essential life within. No object without a subject, as Arthur Schopenhauer (1788-1860) said. This cannot come from merely relishing all the sensual pleasures of the world. It involves the biological evolution of the rich and subtle mind, automatically entailing a curb on worldly urges. We should not forget that, as Søren Kierkegaard (1813-1855) puts it, "man is a synthesis of the temporal and the Eternal but predestined to live in the world." No total withdrawal into a monk's cell or the ivory tower should be contemplated, however tempting it may seem in a capricious world.[58] The competitive capitalism that envelops and consumes must be made to serve, not to dominate.

The body needs its sustenance of food and drink. The soul, too, needs food and drink, and this sustenance must also come from the outside.

---

[54] J. C. Cooper 1981, p. 10.

[55] The placebo effect of therapy is discussed by J. Horgan 1999, pp. 86-91.

[56] Freud's theories reflect his time and origin and offer much for the understanding of mental aberrations but little for a happy life. L. L. Whyte 1979, p. 68 and p. 74.

[57] A. de Saint-Exupéry (1900-1944) says in a similar fashion, "One does not see well except with the heart, the essence is invisible to the eyes" (On ne voit bien qu'avec le coeur, l'essentiel est invisible pour les yeux). In *Le Petit Prince*, quoted in W. Heisenberg 1974, p. 69.

[58] "It is equally wrong to become a recluse or to 'follow the crowd'." H. G. Creel 1953, p. 34.

George Bernard Shaw (1856-1950) expresses this masterfully in *Heartbreak House*:

> Ellie: A soul is a very expensive thing to keep: much more so than a motorcar.
> Shotover: Is it? How much does your soul eat?
> Ellie: Oh, a lot. It eats music and pictures and books and mountains and lakes and beautiful things to wear and nice people to be with. In this country you can't have them without a lot of money: that is why our souls are so horribly starved.

How true this dialogue rings! The soul needs sustenance and be fed as much as the body. There has to be the right food at the right time. Man's outer life requires vigilant care; so does his inner life. The one is as valid as the other. One should nurture the things that help maintaining the poised man. In the life of Balance no religion is rejected; on the contrary, religions are welcome.[59] Religious ceremonies can be nourishment. They can serve man – they are the rational expression of inner experience. Doubly rich is the man who blends inner life with church and faith. If the experience is sustained using whatever uplifting means, the entire life can become a happy sacrament.[60] As the Chinese classic, *Chung Yung* says, "When balance and harmony reach the highest point, the whole universe is tranquil and all things flourish."[61]

16. All True Insights from Within

Materialism has grown in the western world as a reflection and result of scientific rationalism. It had its innocent beginnings in ancient Greece, developed slowly through the Middle Ages and became an avalanche with the rise of modern science from about 1600 when Francis Bacon (1561-1626) proclaimed the "scientific method" to be the religion of modern man and Heaven to be progress on Earth. Science and progress made logical clockwork of God's wondrous Creation. Evolution came then to explain everything, including religion. "One by one the old dog-

---

[59] And there are many religions, big and small. They can be amazingly alike but also differ as to traditions, icons, rites, views on afterlife etc. but all bespeak man's inner experience See W. James 1963.

[60] After all, "the various religions are differing styles of doing the same thing." A. W. Watts 1972, p. 170.

[61] Chung Yung, *Doctrine of the Mean*, in: J. Legge 1861-1872.

mas disappeared; the Gothic cathedral of medieval belief, with its delightful details and grotesques, collapsed; the ancient God fell from his throne along with the Bourbons, heaven faded into mere sky, and hell became only an emotional expression."[62]

Already George Herbert (1593-1633), Bacon's contemporary, realised, however, how paltry the new truths were without the inner dimension:

> Philosophers have measured mountains,
> Fathom'd the depths of seas, of states, and kings
> Walk'd with a staffe to heav'n, and traced fountains:
> But there are two vast, spacious things,
> The which to measure it doth those behove:
> Yet few there are that found them: Sinne and Love.[63]

Present-day science is a product of the last two centuries. Since the nineteenth century, attempts have been made even to split the mind into structural units. In its lurch grows atheism, an outgrowth of the ongoing secularisation of the modern world. It is only recently that religious sentiment has crept in again through the back door of the atomic and quantum physics. Religion and science move on different planes, and it is witnessed how science touches religion and religion science. Physicists such as Albert Einstein (1879-1955),[64] Niels Bohr (1885-1962), and Werner Heisenberg (1901-1976) have stood in awe before the wonder of the Whole, ending up with a gnosticism akin to religion. "Science suggests a cosmology; and whatever suggests a cosmology suggests a religion," says Alfred N. Whitehead, and leading physicists agree with him. And Albert Schweitzer (1875-1965) says that "The highest knowledge is to know that we are surrounded by mystery."[65]

---

[62] W. Durant 1953, p. 193.

[63] G. Herbert quoted in H. Baker 1952, p. 25.

[64] Einstein said in *Mein Weltbild* (in translation): "The most beautiful and profoundest that man can experience is the feeling of the mysterious. There are the roots of religion and all deeper striving in art and science. Who has not experienced this seems to me to be, if not dead, to be blind. To feel that there is something, unreachable hidden behind what is experienced, whose beauty and sublimity appear only indirectly as a weak reflection, *THAT* is religiosity. In *THIS* sense I am religious. It is enough for me, amazed and astounded, to feel (*ahnen*) and try humbly to grasp a poor picture (*Abbild*) of the sublime structure of creation." Quoted in F. Herneck 1976, p. 254. From Einstein's *"Mein Glaubensbekenntnis"* (1932).

[65] A. Schweitzer is quoted in H. Wilder Foote 1955, p. 25.

As the scientists set their eyes deeper and deeper into matter, whether the galaxies or the atoms, others direct their eyes deeper and deeper into the human dilemma. In many cases they find satisfaction in descriptions of human beings, caught in the wheels and claws of the machine. Renowned writers like Jean-Paul Sartre (1905-1980), Albert Camus (1913-1960) or Abe Kôbô (1924-1993) seek the meaning of existence. Sartre ends up with a godless reality where man creates his own values and Abe's hero finds meaning discovering water in a sand dune. Camus tells of a universe bereft of divine purpose and "cosmic meaning."[66] The existential nexus remains in the material world. They ignore Socrates who once said: "All true insights come from within."

Objective consciousness has expanded, while subjective consciousness has shrunk. It is easy to understand why conflicts arise between what is conscious and what is subconscious. The deep regions of the mind rejected and driven into oblivion. We live with a Humpty Dumpty dilemma. We have learned to take things apart but do not know how to put them together again.

17. Existentialism and Our Time

It can only be the dehumanised intellectual atmosphere of the second millennium that brings existentialists like Sartre and Camus to the forefront. Our times have also witnessed the Christian existentialism, but how many have heard of Gabriel Marcel (1889-1973) or Paul Claudel (1868-1955)? They are not taken as seriously as Sartre and Camus, perhaps because their existentialist message is anchored in religion, which does not fit the *Zeitgeist*. At a rough guess, while ten out of ten have heard of Sartre and Camus, only one of ten might have heard of Marcel and Claudel. The mass media, paid to follow flux and fashion and to please their audience, are to blame. It is easier to go with the crowd than against it, just as it is easier to swim with the tide than against it. Intel-

[66] Two visits by the writer on the same day in Paris (in 1948), the Notre Dame Church in the morning and an Existentialist café, located in a basement, in the evening opened the eyes of this writer to the soaring light of the one institution and the subterranean darkness of the other.

lectuals, too, rarely move against the trends. It pays. So it is in the East and so it is in the West.

Whether the existentialist reaction has developed an outer or inner aspect, however, it has been a movement against the 'malady of objectivity' of our era. Those who have described the spiritual crisis are numerous, just as those who have taken a stand by voicing philosophical or religious convictions. Their list is long. They constitute a reaction to the entire streamlined and computerised reality we inhabit. It is their great feat to defend the individual and demonstrate the threat to his freedom and uniqueness.

Our world has become rational. Even philosophy "is no longer a way of life, as it was in antiquity." It has become "an exclusively academic affair."[67] This is Jung's conclusion, who says that both theology and philosophy have become "highbrow" and "learned", often without both God and religion. One is not inspired by their obscure jargon that usually exudes light without heat.

18. Modern Reality

Existentialist thinkers have reacted against the modern hubris. It is debatable whether it was Blaise Pascal (1623-1662), William Blake or Søren Kierkegaard who was the first exponent of modern 'existential' philosophy. This thinking has followed the objectivised development as a shadow until this very day.

The existentialist philosophers are on the right track, whether they are inner or outer in their manifold messages. Each and every one of them has something to tell people about the individual and his condition, reminding of flesh and blood, of nerves and loneliness on a globe which wishes to treat all individuals en masse. Our world possesses the means to effectuate this, in this virtual age of the computer.

Despite their number, the thinkers, have failed to disclose a way out of our contemporary materialistic impasse. Confronted with trends, painfully vivid, they revolt against the inhumanity of lifeless and abstract philosophy. By disposition and inclination they are repulsed by

---

[67] C. G. Jung and R. Wilhelm 1957, p. 84.

modern trends, and depict the human predicament with keen sensitivity. They describe the illness and analyse the issues displaying indignation, but rarely demonstrate any new road befitting the modern age. They raise the questions but their replies ring hollow, unsupported as they are by any true transcendent dimension.

19. The Hemingway Way

At our disposal we have existentialist thought that is persistently driving towards greater singularity and is neither acceptable nor recommended. It may seem tempting and very masculine to follow in Ernest Hemingway's (1899-1961) footsteps. It may be thrilling and satisfying to be always on the go, seeking glory and excitement, to be heroic, rebellious and macho, to go to war, to taste the blood of bullfighting, but, more often than not, it ends pathetically in tragedy. Friedrich Nietzsche (1844-1900) might make sense in his quest for a new ethics, asserting that Christianity is the kernel of the ailments of modernity. But he was wrong. He was barking up the wrong tree. It was not the Christian faith that was culpable; it was the new era and its materialism and mechanism that were reprehensible. Hemingway expounded a glorious lifestyle as long as it lasted, but once it was over, it left a void. Depression, angst, alcohol and self-hatred followed one upon another and suicide became the 'heroic' solution. The reason was that his life was unbalanced from the outset. Had it been united with inspired life, it would likely have been less heroic and flamboyant but happier and ended in a better way. One shall remain sceptical when reading the slogan, "I don't want to be happy. I want to be alive and active." This, once again, is the defiant youth, who would rather rush into battle and die than sit back and reason before acting. Heroism had its last stand in the First World War and perhaps in the 1930s when war still seemed romantic. The Second World War put an end to that. Until 1945 man could allow hatred and arrogance to lead all the way to war. The weapons developed at that time exposed any dreams of freedom through action and war to be a sham and a nightmare. The new forces must be bridled, and even charismatic geniuses must refrain from their zeal and learn moderation and strive for perhaps boring but legitimate outlets for their ardour. The hero of old must be tamed to be the balanced gentleman.

Prometheus and Nietzsche's superman are out of date. We are done with the heroic. After many centuries of youthful ventures, man must attain maturity not only in the military sphere but in all fields, ecology and natural resources among others. It might hurt some people of vigour, but it is necessary. We must sublimate and restrain our passions – or we will die entrapped by them.

20. Heroism and Moderation – The Golden Mean

The kind of heroism needed at the present day is the heroism inspired by the heart. Of course, the young should not be bereaved of their ardour and exuberance. Young people must not grow old too soon. Challenge and adventure belong to the young. One would not rob these pleasures from them. Still, juvenile behaviour should not be taught as a creed to mankind, young or old. "To every thing there is a season"[68] and it behooves man as he grows older to shed the habits and inclinations of his youth and act his age, donning the mantle of maturity.

In dealing with people one ought to strive for moderation. The ancient Greeks had the term *maedèn agan* and the Norse the word *lagom* to express that things must have their true proportions. The good lies between two extremes. Both the Chinese and English traditions see the mature person acting in a poised fashion. This is perhaps the reason why the English gentleman and the Chinese scholar alike can seem inscrutable.

Chinese philosophy taught the Golden Mean and Greek philosophy did the same. Both the Greeks and the Chinese realised that the good lies between two extremes. The Romans spoke about the *Via Media*[69] in deeds and words and Confucius stated that "to go to far is as wrong as not going far enough."[70] Among the world's great authors, Shakespeare (1564-1616) was the most successful in manifesting that extremes must be avoided. The British ideal of the gentleman must be product of the long process read about in the Shakespeare. Can there be a more

68 Ecclesiastes, 3: 1.

69 "Middle Way." The Romans said further, "Veritas stat in medio," that is, "truth exists in the middle."

70 *Lun Yü* XI, 15: 3.

charming image of the Mean – and Balance – than Portia in the Merchant of Venice? There she stands as the sublime ideal, always gentle in mirth and sorrow, always ready to help and assist. Perhaps Shakespeare felt that only a woman was suitable to depict such a paragon.

The democratic process can be considered man's noblest and most successful attempt to keep to a mean in politics. Democracy is not perfect but it is certainly restrained in comparison with the alternatives. It offers the Open Society with man at its core. He has the power to decide the future of the land with his single vote at elections. It seems as if Adam Smith's mysterious "invisible hand" is as much behind the democratic political process as behind the free market forces. An unknown hand marks the cards.

Moderation, not asceticism, must be attained. Gluttony and inebriation are no indications of bodily equilibrium. Sad it is that man is created in such a way that he can push his undertakings beyond the bounds and overdo it. He can eat himself into obesity and drink himself into a stupor. He can scrimp and save and he can gorge himself. Like other creatures he is not aware of satiety or when the level of enough is reached. He is capable of overstepping the limit – and he suffers as a result. Sexual urge constitutes no exception. Healthy contentment is what should be striven for, not excess and debauchery. As Lao Tzu sees it:

> If you would not spill the wine,
> Do not fill the glass too full
> If you wish your blade to hold its edge,
> Do not try to make it over-keen.
> If you do not want your house to be robbed,
> Do not fill it with gold and jade.
> Wealth, rank and arrogance add up to ruin,
> As surely as two and two add up to four.
> Such is the Way of Heaven.[71]

21. Conrad and the Jungle of Life

Hence, there are barriers beyond which individualism and freedom from attachment cannot go. A sense of parity must be found, this time

---

[71] *Lao Tzu*, ch. 9.

between private and public lives. The collective strait jacket and regimentation can suffocate the human being and damage initiative and originality irretrievably and too much separation, can lead to desolation and alienation. Joseph Conrad (1857-1924) (in *An Outpost of Progress*): "Few men realize that their life, the very essence of their character, their capabilities and their audacities, are only the expression of their belief in the safety and security of their surroundings. The courage, the composure, the confidence; the emotions and principles; every great and significant thought belongs not to the single person but to the crowd: to the crowd that believes blindly in the irresistible efficacy of its institutions and of its morals, in the power of its police and of its opinion."[72]

He says further,

> To the sentiment of being alone of one's kind, to the clear perception of the loneliness of one's thoughts, of one's sensations – to the negation of the habitual, which is safe, there is added the affirmation of the unusual, which is dangerous; a suggestion of things vague, uncontrollable, and repulsive, whose discomposing intrusion excites the imagination and tries the civilized nerves of the foolish and the wise alike.[73]

Conrad's starting place certainly is an abode in the jungle, but what is the difference between the true jungle and the modern city with its cutthroat competition? Is it not a fact that one can be more 'alone' in the hustle-and-bustle of a city than in the vacuous calm of the remote countryside? In the social jungle everyone is as much a prey as in the true jungle.

One can develop loneliness and existential angst to the same extent in the midst of a crowd and an unhappy social context as in the middle of a forest. Either place can be detrimental to health and welfare. Rimbaud (1854-1891) in the West and Li Po (ca. 701-762) in the East make it clear that extreme individualism is destructive. They are fascinating, the Rimbauds and Li Pos, just as apparently war is more fascinating than peace. However, who wants to see his own son or daughter to move into a life of debauchery or going into war? The fact is that most men and women need social institutions and friendly relations for orderly living; separated from good relationships they may end up crying out like one of Con-

---

[72] J. Conrad 1898, p. 122.

[73] *Ibid.*

rad's characters: "The horror! The horror" as he finds himself alone with his fate in the jungle of Congo. Conrad describes the death-in-life of a man entirely isolated from society, encircled by the jungle on all sides.

22. The Private and the Public

Since time immemorial man has thus been a group animal, existing and hunting in a flock. As a member of a pack of 'wolves' he can be seen moving throughout the millennia and right into modern times. Even in this day he is a group member, to which most achievements bear witness, and he suffers when he leaves the group and becomes a Steppenwolf, a lone wolf. The question is whether the loneliness found so often today is not due in part to the fact that he has departed from the unity of the collective, to which he once belonged.

Historically, both East and West, the family has been at the centre of man's life. In China it is the very heart of ethical thought whether Confucian or Neo-Confucian. A small family is often not enough, rather a greater family or a village. Often enough one bears witness to the warm atmosphere in large families and, correspondingly, how the cordial atmosphere and intimacy often diminish with small families. One can ask oneself whether the term loneliness even existed in the course of time when everyone belonged to his flock or family. Above all one can forward the question as to the role of the private car, the big splitter-up of mankind, in creating lonely people.

A family is still most fitting for private life. Private should not denote that one lives the life of the loner, and collective should not imply some large social monstrosity beyond our comprehension. If private and collective are seen in a family perspective, they form a sound continuum. To be all alone is dangerous, as Joseph Conrad said; to be engulfed in a nationwide collective is also dangerous. Both corporate and individual lives must be afforded their periodic changes of life.

Extreme emphasis on individualism can be considered to be a part of the defiance and revolt that is displayed by many existentialist thinkers in their lives and writings. It is not a sign of a mind in balance. At times they take such delight in their own rebellion that it borders on narcissism and is close to mental disorder.

23. Rebellion, Science and Western Defiance

Rebellion is not a manifestation of a mind in balance. One fist punching Heaven has been a symbol of western culture for as long as we can think back. We read about it in the Old Testament and the Greek tragedies. This youthful attitude is yet prevalent in this day. What is more, it is now exported to all corners of the globe and hardly a day passes without bombs or revolts.

The history of the antagonism between nature and man has its roots in the Near East and the Bible demanding that man subdue, control and exploit the earth (*Genesis,* 1: 28). This demand came from Palestine as an integral part of the Christian religion and has influenced the West through a couple of millennia and now practically all mankind. In Europe this trend became especially evident in the wake of the Reformation. The religious piety that existed in the medieval view of life vanished gradually as worldly life became dominant.

This new *Weltgeist* offered ample room for greed and gold to gain the upper hand. Mammon and avidity brought the Europeans out on the oceans, discovering new lands. Blatant rapacity in internecine European competition led from the Portuguese and Spanish thalassocracies to the British and Dutch thalassocrasies which dominated the world for centuries. Not much religion was left when the Portuguese or Spanish met the British and Dutch on the high seas and they burned and killed each other – always in the name of God.

The defiant posture has, however, driven man onward from victory to victory. It has led him into the atom and up to the moon; now it takes him beyond the sun and into the expanding universe. He has the globe in his hands and he has improved his lot. The scientific enquiry by means of inductive observation and experimentation has widened and enriched his views on cosmos and Creation.[74]

---

[74] See R. H. Torrance 1994, pp. 273-277.

24. Chance or Plan

Balance in life is a sign of Chance in action. Doors open up and opportunities present themselves. It is almost as if the entire universe leagues up and embraces a person and shows him the way. As soon as conscious effort is involved, it is no longer the same thing. The mind must be still, withdrawn to the zero point where the inner logic is at play and inner and outer are one. Clarity resplends, miracles occur and divine wisdom acts in unexpected ways. Everyone has experienced this phenomenon, when something has happened that cannot be explained by common logic; it is brushed off and, just like dreams in the night, soon forgotten. These fleeting glimpses of serenity should not be swept away into oblivion so rashly, because they are manifestations of one's being in tune with the wonder of inner consciousness. They are 'occult' as one great thinker concluded after such an experience. They should be remembered. They are joy in life. Life is poor without them.

How many of today's depressions would be avoided if only the inner were allowed to dictate and people stopped longing for objects which do not give a true value to life! Realizing that Chance functions in their lives, they sense that they are in harmony with the depths of Being. What need then for religious dogmas and churches?

Planned life stands in sharp contrast to the life of Chance. It might be easier but less fulfilling. It is digital versus analogue. Digital routine is prevalent presently, when a person can as well be at the wrong place at the wrong time, and relish a flat screen rather than enjoy the panorama beyond the screen. He may achieve a sense of detachment from the world and feel deceptively free. Only facing outwards, he is not. He is the robot and the slave of the moment.[75]

"Alles [ist] Zufall (Chance)," says S. Klein, "All is Chance." It is Klein's conclusion that all existences display the miracle of Chance.[76] Thus also individual life. Quantum physicists have conceived a supracausal (in)determinism, not agreeing with Newtonian determinism, rather denoting Chance working at the sub-atomic level – and over the Whole.

---

[75] W. Blake 1995, p. 45.

[76] See S. Klein 2004, in toto. "Miracle is faith's dearest child," says Goethe.

25. Inner Chance and Outer Balance

Chance is there to serve man. In all Creation, the vital spirit comes from the inside and man is no exception. If these inner impulses are followed in both easy and difficult situations, one need not go wrong. One often does when one allows the world to direct one's life and actions.

Chance, thus, enters from the Eternal and Balance refers to the resulting order. The driving thrust proceeds from the inside to the outside, not in the other direction. Man is inclined to believe in his newfangled pride that he participates in the Creation, but his participation will never be more than "pebbles on the shore of an infinite ocean" (Newton), and his actions will often not be for the better. Worse still, man's intrusion might endanger man's future on Earth and even mean the death of all. It is certainly best that man does not meddle with Chance. Like the Greeks he should keep in mind that Destiny ultimately decides.

It is important to recognise that the emotive and the cognitive, sentiment and intellect, are complementary parts of the human psyche. They function best as a unity. Man is given the intellect for a good reason. He must follow his inner voice but not ignore his intellect. The inner should show the way but reason and common sense must see that self-delusion and imagination are averted. Rational knowledge need not be in opposition to intuitive knowledge. The legal system of a country must be there, changing as times change. When a country like Germany has 55.000 laws and regulations in its legal system it is an example of human reason at work.

As Marcus Aurelius says, "Without this Inner Cause, which dictates both action and inaction, the body is of no more use than the weaver's shuttle without a weaver, the writer's pen without a writer, or the coachman's whip without a horse and carriage."[77]

26. Balance and Happiness is for Everyone

Each and every human person is unique and has to accomplish his own equilibrium. Balance exists at as many levels as there are human be-

---

[77] In J. Star 1991, p. 106.

ings. Intensity varies. A person of high intensity presides over a level of Balance that is easily disturbed and requires constant attention. Another individual of low intensity comes into this world at a level hardly requiring any attention at all. His existence is uncomplicated and he can be envied by the highstrung person, who lives with a constant awareness of an implosion. Those who are born with low emotional capacity come in great numbers. For those born with passionate fervour, something that usually goes hand in hand with other strong sentiments, require considerably more effort to achieve Balance. It can be a long struggle lasting until the energy abates in life's autumn. The 'sharp' person is more vulnerable than the 'dense' person, who, on the whole, maintains his mental health easily and is, generally, closer to the warmth of feelings. We envy those who empathise with others, who are more outgoing and display their sympathy for suffering and misery readily.

The opposite end of the spectrum would be the individual who is indifferent and distant and views the world and his fellow men and women through a glass door or the visor of an iron mask. Indeed there are as many personality types as there are individuals, and therefore we cannot demand that there should be a strait jacket imposed on everyone! This has generally been the mistake of the established religions, which with the vanity of the creeds have tried to cut each person on a Procrustean bed to the same size. The general way inwards to the absolute truth should be indicated – but no more. Navigation and design of the route is a matter of personal choice. The experience lies solely within the individual. As it is said: "Let each man be his own conscience and his own church."

27. Balance is Private

The directing of the eyes inwards and achieving Balance has the great advantage of being a private affair. No confession is involved. No church is needed. Priests and gurus are sidelined. Absolution is irrelevant. Spiritual imbalance can be corrected instantly. If successful, it is lived in privacy, and if unsuccessful, it is also lived in privacy. Sensation and experience bear witness to success or failure. The cognition is inside one's own heart and mind. One need not search for it in particular places or with regard to others. Just as one need not search for it in creeds, ethical codes, tenets and cults as there are ten in a penny! "The fault, dear Brutus, is not in our stars, but in ourselves," says Shakespeare's Cassius.[78]

This equipoise has another advantage. It bears no ill-will and rarely arouses jealousy. As soon as an institutional church and its dogma are established to accommodate the private experience, one can anticipate antagonism, criticism, persecution and inquisition. But as long as the experience is at the private level in solitude, there will be little to react against – it is as silent outside as it is inside.

Balance leads to a smiling face. And a smiling face can work wonders, engendering a younger countenance and contented relations with all living things. Balanced people are generally open to the world. They seek no enemies. Their faces reflect it, and others are infected by their gaiety. A stern, dour, official face, on the other hand, makes no one happy.

A culture yearns for people radiating joy and merriment and it makes life easier to live both for themselves and others. A day without joyous laughter is a lost day!

It must be recognised that each being is born with his personality, and that people are not cast-iron copies or cloned sheep. Respect should be the beginning and end of association with other people.

My happiness is shared happiness! My personal equanimity finds reflection in others around me, my friends, acquaintances, family, neighbours, colleagues! I do not exist in a social vacuum! It does not take a Buddhist to realise that I am others and others are me!

28. Intuition

Inner Balance implies an attitude of mind that prevails in harmony with the entire universe. This attitude manifests itself in the manner with which one deals with things. When one exists at the existential midpoint one knows when to act or when not to. Call it inspiration, intuition or foresight coming from the conjunction of feeling and reason. It is not just outer reason that makes the decision, but as much omnipotent and omniscient providence. Neither of the two is predominant; at the exis-

[78] *Julius Caesar*, Act I, Scene 2. In W. Shakespeare 1937, p. 862.

tential still point of the heart, they are mutually important. Where the two meet, true life begins.

In such a way, one brings in the totality of one's person, freeing oneself from the entanglements of the world. Decisions made under such conditions may seem without rhyme or reason, but it belongs to experience that what seems unreasonable at first may later seem quite reasonable. Most difficult is to follow inspiration when mundane considerations signal another direction and dare to act when the entire society tells one not to. The dare pays off in the long run. To be right at the wrong time is difficult, but one is vindicated when the right time comes.

In *Yet Being Someone Other* L. van der Post says: "Intuition is, I believe, a natural capacity in all living things to see around the corners of the future. ..." Van der Post is "acutely conscious of how the natural walls of awareness had never been opaque but strangely transparent, as if bombarded by some X-ray light or cathode lamp of a mystery flame from beyond." He could never ignore "those strange events, like the working of chance and affects which the long arm of coincidence often lobbed over those oddly luminous walls, and which could not be left out of any honest evaluation of reality." Van der Post shows in his writings that he has been "subjected to a genuine premonition of the future" and that strange contingencies have led him from event to event. He "has acquired an immense respect for coincidences of any kind." He does have, however, "a strange feeling of unease" when recounting chains of events which have an occult flavour.[79] This is natural in this secular age when anything in the least "occult" is associated with darkness and superstition.

29. Intuition and Minimalism

It would be for the better in our overactive world if only acts inspired by intuition were carried out. On the personal, national and international levels it would suffice to execute only the decisions deriving from the interior Will and conviction.

Paradoxically, the more one discards the world, the more one becomes part of it! Generally speaking, problems dissolve naturally and

[79] L. van der Post 1982, p. 168.

conflicts vanish. It would also be in our interest if the race for more and more and for ever higher living standard was checked by an appraisal of the actual needs. Such moves might be damaging to industry and result in fewer cars on our streets, but it would certainly spell a healthier society. The ideal in every field should be to acquire what is needed and to do what is required. Neither less nor more.

One cannot always follow Epicurus' maxim[80] to "live unknown" but one can endeavour to be known as little as possible. In the same manner one can strive after living penniless and taciturn but a few pennies and words are needed. "Man cannot live by bread alone," says the Bible – but he cannot live without bread either! The ideal and goal is that one can be happy with little and sing Gershwin's "I Got Plenty o' Nuttin' an' Nuttin's Plenty fo' Me."[81]

One undoubtedly feels better when little is desired and when what is done is deeply intuited and apprehended. When one's heart reigns, the world is in no state of chaos, and one's life is neither senseless nor purposeless. When in our day people speak of the chaos of the world, it is, more often than not, a reflection of their own chaotic mental lives. If you are disorderly inwards, you find things equally disorderly outwards, and you exacerbate the situation by starting out on the wrong foot. It might be everyone's experience that things go wrong and that one runs into all kinds of obstacles, when one is out of poise. Equally, it might be everyone's experience that everything seems to fall into place and run smoothly, when one sets out in the good mood of a happy conscience. One is received, as one comes. If you are in Balance you are everyone; if you are off Balance, you are nobody.

30. In the Lucky Moment

The ancient Greeks had the expression, *en te tuxe agate*. It can be translated as "in the lucky moment." With these words, they expressed that there is a lucky and right moment for everything. This concept is far removed from our contemporary intellectual world, but it was quite clear

---

[80] Epicurus (341-270 B.C.), Greek realist philosopher who stood for moderation in private life and liberal humanism in political life.

[81] In Gershwin's (1898-1937) *Porgy and Bess*.

to the Greeks. Their reality included the supernatural and as natural to them as the rational world is to modern man. They viewed things upon a wide scale that modern man has reduced to consciousness. He has impoverished himself by laying the emphasis on objects which can be measured, weighed and quantified, forsaking the wisdom of his heart.[82] Trapped in a universe that is cold and aimless, he tends to talk about the 'cosmic vacuity' – and no wonder, when he leads the one-dimensional life of the 'outer man', not matched by the life of the 'inner man.'[83]

The parity of inner and outer life is essential. The inner dimension must balance the outer dimension. As Albert Einstein says, "Science without religion is lame; religion without science is blind."[84] He says further, "He who is foreign to this feeling [of the Eternal], who cannot stop in wonder and be struck by awe, he is close to dead; his eyes are closed."[85]

In Balance we dwell in an infinite symmetry. There is a lucky moment, a good moment for an action and it lies with the individual being to grasp this moment. It cannot be explained logically, but a person who lives at ease in heart and soul feels and knows the right time for a decision. Each cell seems to tell him when the "happy confluence of circumstances"[86] has come and he is in the right place at the right time.[87]

This is equivalent to the 'good knowledge' in Chinese philosophy. The Will furthers and enhances the Balance and it is wise to follow its dictates. Actually, a decision is not a decision when it follows the inner guidance. People suffer, when they ignore and disobey what it tells them to do. This neglect may ruin their lives – should they not have a second chance. Louis Pasteur (1822-1895) describes this moment of bliss:

---

82 "The wisdom and mysticism of the East ... should remind us of that which is familiar in our own culture and which we have already forgotten, and we should direct our attention to that which we have pushed aside as insignificant, namely the fate of *our inner man*," says C. G. Jung. Quotation in N. W. Ross 1966, p. 9.

83 "Nature becomes a dull affair, soundless, scentless, colourless; merely the hurrying of material, endlessly, meaninglessly, in the abysses of space." D. Loy 2000, p. 71.

84 A. Einstein, quoted in R. Stark 2003, p. 197.

85 A. Einstein, quoted in I. Hedenius 1964, p. 90.

86 C. Berlinski 2006, p. 70.

87 "It is reasonable to suppose that every cell that goes to constitute the body has its own consciousness", says Carveth Read (1848-1931).

> I see everywhere in the world the inevitable expression of the concept of infinity ... The idea of God is nothing more than one form of the idea of infinity. So long as the riddle of the divine beyond weighs on the human mind, so long will temples be raised to the cult of the infinite, whether it be called *Brahman*, *Yahweh* or *Allah* ... The Greeks understood the occult *élan*,[88] of the esoteric side of things. They bequeathed to us one of the noblest words of our language, 'enthusiasm' – *en theos* – "God within" or "in God" – which means being possessed by a power greater than oneself. The grandeur of personal actions is assessed by the inspiration from which they spring. Happy is he who bears a God within, and who obeys it. The ideals of art, of science, are lighted by reflection from the infinite.[89]

31. The Mystical and the Transcendental

The world of literature is brimming with depictions of visions, peak experiences, miracles and wonders, even in our day and age. At times it almost seems as though many authors seek what they label 'mystical'.[90] The occult must be there before they are content. They do not see, nor hear, nor smell, nor taste nor feel the wonders around them! All life is wonder! The greatest wonder of all: to be alive![91]

Our time is crying out for the demystification of the divine. Things beyond should be made as natural as they were for the medieval Europeans and eastern peoples. People are besieged by wondrous events; they must recognise them as such and let them enrich their psychic life. They have merely to acknowledge that the thither world is as real as the hither world, that there is a Grand Equilibrium of complementary halves, one half being eternal and the other half being temporal.

---

88 L. L. Whyte writes about the "*élan* which moves us, the active principle which leads us to feel, to imagine, to judge, to think and to act. This is more than mechanics, or dynamics, or chance." L. L. White 1979, p. 70. Christ says, "The Kingdom of Heaven is in the midst of you."

89 A. Koestler 1971, p. 254.

90 The terms "mystical" and "mysticism" are avoided in this work because they carry connotations of occultism, magic and delusion in the modern West. Terms, such as, 'inner', 'spiritual', 'spirituality' and 'innerness' are used instead. In pre-Cartesian Europe and the East intuition, spirituality and mysticism were considered *natural*, not unnatural. It is worth noting that the word *Mystik* with occult connotations is first found in the German tradition in 1760 and the French term *la mystique* is found only a little earlier in France.

91 "Take wonder away – and there is little left!"

The two halves converge in the heart of the psyche and constitute the Balance of the mind. It remains, then, people's duty to cultivate both sides of the equilibrium. They must be attentive to and enhance their birth acquisitions by reflection, meditation, not forgetting prayer. None of these need be strict and regimented as ascribed by teachers or priests. It can be short intervals at any time in daily work when the mind turns inward and enjoys the happy moment that passes by, bringing inner peace during the day and good sleep at night.

Inner experiences are valuable, but to lead a simple and contented life on the axis between the Eternal and the Temporal is enough. No further revelation is necessary. Heaven need not be mentioned and God need not be discussed. Theology is superfluous. It does not matter whether the experience is immanent or transcendent and relates to something or nothing. What does this matter once the Balance is achieved and a happy harmony pervades body and soul? When "I within doth flow with seas of life, like wine."[92]

32. William Blake and His Laughing Song

Poet and visionary William Blake described this inner state of being. He gave it the name "The Songs of Innocence and of Experience (1789 and 1794), which dwells with Wisdom." In these 'Songs' he describes Innocence as the moment of spontaneous laughter when the whole of nature laughs in response:

When the green woods laugh with the voice of joy,
And the dimpling stream runs laughing by,
And the air does laugh with our merry wit
And the green hill laughs with the noise of it."

When the meadows laugh with lively green,
And the grasshopper laughs in the merry scene,
When Mary and Susan and Emily
With their sweet round mouths sing 'Ha, Ha, He!'

When the painted birds laugh in the shade,
Where our table with cherries and nuts is spread,

[92] Thomas Traherne (1637?-1674) in a poem, "Wonder."

> Come live, and be merry, and join with me,
> To sing the sweet chorus of 'Ha, Ha, He!'[93]

Walt Whitman describes the same harmony with the words, "I am satisfied ... I see, dance, laugh, sing."[94]

How true! When our Inner knows and senses Balance, it manifests itself as exhilaration bursting all bounds and collapsing into laughter, dance and song. Nature joins in, and one is one with all reality. Good laughter is a sign of a cheerful disposition; when it dies out, it is a sign of ennui and alienation, of mental and physical discomfort. The serious mood may also indicate Balance and be appropriate in many situations. When the mind explodes in mirth, song, dance and laughter, people can deride you and you do not care. One is not entirely happy about it, but one takes it in stride; something that one does not take easily when one's heart is upset. It follows that this is a time when one laughs playfully at everything. At times when natural warmth is lacking and external rectitude is important, a cheerful face is not always welcome. One has, unfortunately, to restrain spontaneous joy – and refrain from outbursts of happy laughter. Merriment, however, hurts no one, it is infectious, creating rapport! It is also said that the essence of love is laughter and happiness! The same can be said about good humour which goes hand in hand with happiness. And "luck comes to those who laugh," says a Japanese proverb.

33. Balance Equals Peace of Mind. Balance is All

A term that corresponds to Balance is 'peace of mind'. One tends to use peace of mind to refer to the same kind of mental situation and the two terms can be considered synonymous. F. J. Sheen's term 'the peace of soul' is also synonymous but puts more emphasis on inwardness.[95] The three expressions refer to the same inner state. It may be tempting to dream of a Balance or peace of mind or peace of soul that persists in contemplative stillness and absolute bliss, but a person is not born to remain in a vegetative state like a plant, merely enjoying the serene feeling. Bal-

[93] W. Blake 1995, p. 27.
[94] W. Whitman 1959, p. 27.
[95] See F. J. Sheen 1951, in toto.

ance culminates in socio-cultural activity, leads from internal ineffable experience to external direct knowledge.

In his book 'Zen and the Art of Motorcycle Maintenance' Pirsig formulates this situation quite neatly: "Peace of mind isn't at all superficial, really... It's the whole thing. That which produces it is good maintenance; that which disturbs it is poor maintenance. What we call workability of the machine of nature is just an objectification of this peace of mind. The ultimate test is always your own serenity. If you do not have this when you start and maintain it while you're working, you're likely to build your personal problems right into the machine itself."[96]

It truly depends on your serenity whether you deal correctly with the 'machine.' Once your frame of mind and your activities form one straight line, you can be sure of your being on the right road.

The ancient Greeks recognised Destiny even above Zeus which means that they recognised an ultimate Balance determining things. Destiny is found in the cosmic Balance, likewise in the Balance of all animate life and in man's moral life. In the end Balance and Destiny belong together.

34. The Serene Mind

A mind at peace is in a position to learn, give and take. An unstable mind, on the other hand, is not capable of enquiring acutely about matters and generating new and original thoughts and ideas. The truly great ventures arise spontaneously from the serene mind. One does not ask for them, just receives them. No one can make a request for ideas or inspiration, they simply occur. When we push our wishes, we end up with little or nothing.

Over-involvement in the pettiness of everyday existence inevitably entails the exclusion from significant participation in great pursuits. The proper way is to cultivate the heart and mind and ask for nothing. Then one will surely find that unexpected opportunities will come, and more than one ever dreamed of. Do not make the mistake of pushing doors open, rather wait for them to open. And if they do not, just wait for

[96] R. M. Pirsig 1974, pp. 158-159.

other doors and the right doors for you! Simply be ready! Is it not said that everything works for the patient and attentive mind? From the standpoint of a cold mechanistic world full of callous relations and distractions this may seem improbable and impossible. Hinderances and obstacles are numerous. Nonetheless, the world offers openings for the individual who has few desires and is free from attachments. While holding on to what is within, circumstances will work for him, refresh his spirit and satisfy his mind.[97] This will bear no disappointments since there are no demands. Should something fail to realise, one moves on, free and ready for new opportunities. As the Tibetan proverb goes, "To know how to be satisfied is to hold a treasure in the palm of one's hand."

35. One Line Inwards and Outwards

Life is not always easy. We are constricted by an environment of relations. One is trapped in their middle, and one cannot exist without them. How simple life would be if there were no social relationships! Most people have no choice but to deal with public situations day in day out. Fortunate the person who has only a few acquaintances (the lighthouse keeper)! A good life requires, however, as much social life as solitude. Too much or too little of either throws man out of balance. As Confucius says, "Excess is as bad as deficiency" and "Overcooked is as bad as undercooked."[98] Too much money can be as deleterious to human happiness as too little money.[99] The life of the hermit is no more commendable than the life of social whirl. Either dehumanises man. It should not be indulgence to be alone nor should it be a luxury to socialise. No matter which way one looks at it, the middle road is to be preferred.

What is recommended is a prolongation of the line mentioned above. As the line must be straight at the personal level, it must be straight in social intercourse. Whenever one's association is forthright, coming from one's heart, it is reflected in the honest look accompanied by frank and kind behaviour. Only sincere association counts. Few look forward to formal gatherings; still, on occasions, one is obliged to play the social

---

[97] *Lao Tzu*, ch. 5.

[98] *Lun Yü* X: 7.

[99] If you are a millionaire in happiness, what is the need for much money?

role. However uncomfortable one may feel, one makes one's best to be friendly and sociable. This is appreciated, and when not, there is always a way out. He who retreats from what is twisted is no coward. This should be done before the situation gets out of hand, the emotions rise high and conflict overwhelms. There are always other places and other people. Courts and lawyers are then superfluous and negative emotions nipped in the bud.

Life is too short for warped liaisons. When malice and iniquity invade your world, recall Coriolanus' words: "There is a world elsewhere!"[100]

36. Capacity for both Good and Evil

Two people should align in a relationship that derives from their hearts. Just as both sender and receiver must be on the same wave length in the world of radios, human relations must meet in mutual empathy. This is the way it should be when two people interact. Marriage is the best example: two people ideally on the same wave length. All relationships should similarly disclose intimacy, resembling an Indra's net of shining jewels, everything linked together and integrated. In Indian and Chinese parlance every part contains the Whole. "One subject now knows itself as the part and knows itself as the whole;" "All in one, one in all," as is also said in Chinese classics.

Unfortunately man is born selfish and greedy. In this respect he differs from the rest of nature. Perhaps selfishness was once necessary to survive in harsh surroundings – in caves and wilderness. The acquisition of the bare essentials in terms of food, clothes and shelter required a selfish mind. Within the tribe, or later within the clan or family, perhaps the rate of self-seeking was reduced but, unfortunately, contemporary man is more or less the same as the early caveman who had to struggle for existence. He displays the same egotism in all ventures, resulting in hatred, poisoned hearts, conflicts and wars. History inspires horror: there are no two pages without bloodshed!

---

[100] *Coriolanus*, Act III. In W. Shakespeare 1937, p. 844.

Is it not true to say that power, money and position can make even the most honourable individual drive to perform acts of cruelty toward his fellow beings?

The world is in dire need of 'egoless' people whose warm simplicity and spontaneity constitute the salt of a society. They even up all the greed and envy that surround man. The Samaritan is needed as in Biblical times.

As if egotism were not enough of a bane, man is the master in the arts of hypocracy and duplicity, finding no end of reasons for being self-indulgent. Social order and peace require that personal ambitions are kept to absolute necessity and wants to a modest minimum. This can only be achieved if selfhood is reduced, and desires are minimised. As the Chinese twelfth-century philosopher Chu Hsi writes, "For nourishing the mind, there is nothing better than to have few desires."[101] There is blessing in minimum.

As long as striving and desire are inspired, they are genuine. If not, they lose their sincerity and warmth, ending in unreliability and dishonesty. With introspection one ascertains whether they enhance or diminish life. Outer impression and inner inspiration must harmonise and balance.

37. Sound Relations

There is no better food for the heart and mind than sound relations and there is nothing more disruptive than conflicts and frictions, not to mention outright warfare, both in the social and military sense.

Unfortunately, there are situations which one cannot run away from – "walls you cannot get over or round." Whatever the situation, positive or negative, the best course is to maintain the Balance and face things openly and frankly as they come. This requires strength but it irons out conflicts and pours oil on troubled water. It provides the individual with the strength of character to face the collisions of life. Such situations test the mettle of Balance. When tackling a problem fearlessly deriving

[101] Lao Tzu (ca. 604-531 B.C.) says, "The sage has no ambitions; therefore he has no failures." Chuang Tzu (ca. 300 B.C.) says, "Keep your expenditures low and lessen your desires, ... and you will have enough." Ch. 20.

strength from the inner, with no chip on his shoulder and with no malice in his heart, he becomes detached, pays attention to all aspects, detects the true problem and acts positively. Things become clear, making it possible to dilute over-inflated issues and focus on what is important. Adopting a sympathetic understanding, he places other people in the centre. In such a situation he never harms another person's ego, and he extends his sincere apologies in case the other person does take offence.

There are not only the common five senses but also the extra sense that people so often forget about in the intellectual world: the humour. Humour transcends barriers. No problem need be unsolved if wit and laughter are applied. In a playful perspective, problems turn small.

Not only external stimuli affect the course and progress of mental life. As important are the stimuli which come from within.[102] It is essential that we recognise the inner world with its stunning scope as vast as the ever changing outer world extending before our eyes. Men and women have begun to comprehend, what they felt naturally before, that the conscious ego is seamlessly united with the irrational unconscious; the finite links with the infinite. What comes from the inside, influences as much as what emanates from the outside, and a mature body-mind composite can only be achieved as a reflection of this heightened introspective awareness. Black moods do not necessarily result from stimuli from the exterior world; they can as well depend on stimuli from the inside. The same can be said about white moods. Stimulation can come from either side!

38. René Descartes and Blaise Pascal

In the wake of medieval scholasticism, the Reformation opened society to individualism and discoveries in science that moved the West ahead of the rest of the world. The interior rapport was gradually neglected as the mind's mirror began primarily to reflect what came from the senses.[103] The separation of faith and reason owes its origin to Descartes (1596-

[102] As Dostoevsky said: "Man needs the unfathomable and the infinite just as much as he does the small planet which he inhabits." R. E. Leakey 1981, p. 20.

[103] John Locke (1632-1704) declared that *percipi* were not innate but derived from experience and G. Berkeley (1685-1753) said, "Esse est percipi."

1650), who declared that only 'clear and distinct' ideas could be true. Reality was divided into *res cogitans*, 'conscious substance', and *res extensa*, 'space-occupying substance'. This 'Cartesian dualism' equipped man with blinkers so that his knowledge was reduced to what the five senses and reason could proffer.[104] His psyche became an adding machine rather than a heart and a soul. God was not denied (Descartes was a Catholic believer) but put on pedestal above his Creation and became a matter of devotion. The domain of philosophy was diminished as human endeavours were confined within the physical order. Man was split and he has suffered from mental division, akin to schizophrenia, ever since religion was restricted to faith.[105]

It is a coincidence that Descartes' contemporary and opponent, Blaise Pascal, was, in a sense, the first existentialist. He also belonged to the rise of modern science but he was also devout and recognised that man possessed not only a rational and mathematical mind – *l'esprit de géometrie* – but also a subtle and intuitive mind – *l'esprit de finesse.*[106] Man is both animal and angel. Through personal experiences, Pascal realised that there was an eternal that filled his soul. "His heart has its reasons, which mind knows not." In his work *Pensées* he demonstrates his deep religiosity. He criticised Descartes who had used God as a creator and then banished him from his Creation.[107] He himself renounced material life in favour of devotion to God.

Descartes and Pascal can be regarded as precursors of ages to come, one leading to the Age of Enlightenment (ca. 1660-1800) and the other to modern existentialist thinking. Their roots, in turn, can be traced to the scholastic thought in the thirteenth, fourteenth and fifteenth centuries.

---

[104] Hence Descartes may be blamed for the impasse in which western thought has been caught over the last three centuries. It is said that Cartesianism came in a dream on a cold winter night in 1619. The transcendent other side became "a dark illimitable ocean" (J. Milton, 1608-1674) and God the great "paradox" (S. Kierkegaard). The holy Grail became the hot porridge around which philosophers have circulated ever since like the proverbial fox without touching it.

[105] For this development, see, for example, H. B. Parkes 1970, pp. 280-298, and W. Heisenberg 1959, pp. 130-131.

[106] He expressed, "The silence of these infinite spaces frightens me", in French: "Le silence éternel de ces espaces infinis m'effraye", in B. Pascal 1995, p. 73 in Levi's translation.

[107] É. Gilson 1941, p. 88.

39. Immanuel Kant and Arthur Schopenhauer

Spiritual life came to seem elusive and illusory, since it was not open to verification under a microscope. Later philosophers deemed mind to be something more than a passive mirror of the senses. For Immanuel Kant (1724-1804) it was an actively operating mirror. In spite of his doctrine of the limitation of human reason, he never denied intuition in his philosophy and sought a unified nature. He recognised noumena (*Ding-an-sich*) beyond the 'wall' and an inner voice serving injunctions to be realised in moral life.[108] The two-way traffic between stimuli from the inside and the world outside, entered his philosophy as laws of nature which man is obliged not to interfere with. We not only know but also *feel* that such and such action is right or wrong. He said that "the starry heavens above him and the moral law within him" filled him with awe and respect for Creation on the one hand and a reverent attitude toward life on the other.

Arthur Schopenhauer (1788-1860) followed up on Kant, propounding that reality has its core in noumenal love and empathy more so than in Kantian ethics and rationality. He recognised a Will in the universe as well as in the world of man and was surprised to discover that his reflections coincided with Hinduist and Buddhist thought. He drew parallels between his own arguments and theirs. Consequently, he became aware that eastern and western thinking were akin, the former more noumenal and the latter more phenomenal. After him followed Friedrich Nietzsche whose nihilism was paired with the thought of eternal recurrence, and finally Karl Marx (1818-1883) with militant atheism.

The rationalists and empiricists generally put the prime emphasis on the phenomenal and observable reality. Whether through reason or as empirical fact it concerned this world. Today's analytical thought is no different. It looks at the inside from the outside. What cannot be verified scientifically is relegated to the realm of superstition and darkness.

However rational and empiricist, philosophers rarely denied religion. The most tolerant among political philosophers, John Locke (1632-

---

[108] This was Kant's *Categorical Imperative*. L. Wittgenstein expressed this awe and respect when he said, "Not *how* the world is, is the mystical, but *that* it is." (I. Berlin 1996, p. 176) Kant considered mathematics and physics to be the knowledge beyond which human apprehension could not extend.

1704), ended up saying, "Lastly, those are not to be tolerated who deny the being of God."[109] Even the most sceptical among sceptics, David Hume (1711-1776), who questioned religion's foundation in reason in his *A Treatise of Human Nature* (1739-1740), added that "The whole frame of nature bespeaks an intelligent author; and no rational enquirer can, after serious reflection, suspend his belief for a moment with regard to the primary principles of Theism and Religion."[110] And in the *Of the Original Contract* he says, "All events in the universe are conducted by an uniform plan, and directed to wise purposes."[111]

40. Sigmund Freud, Carl Gustav Jung

Sigmund Freud and Carl Gustav Jung (1875-1961) have evinced that there are mental landscapes beyond the conscious, immense hidden vistas, not seen by the eye, nor sensed by the mind, which influence human life.[112]

Freud focused on questions which usually belong to religion and theology. He penetrated the unconscious and came close to man's heart and soul. He never went deeper in – as did his follower Jung – but established psychoanalysis as a new rational field of study of inner matters. This

[109] In "Letter Concerning Toleration", 1689.

[110] Leon Wieseltier in the International Herald Tribune, 18-19 February 2006, p. 7, discussing Daniel C. Dennet's *Breaking the Spell*. Hume represents the intellectual theist (deist) religion that can be traced through both rationalism and empiricism – and also modern scientism.

[111] D. Hume, *Of the Original Contract*, p. 1. Quotation in M. C. Jacobson 2000, p. 52. Hume said in the *Treatise of Human Nature*, "Reason is, and ought to be, the slave of the passions, and can never pretend to any other office than to serve and obey them." In Part II, 3, 3. Quotation in A. MacIntyre 1966, p, 169.

[112] The senses can reach for a "door in the floor" leading to the lower, dark regions as well as a "door in the ceiling" leading to the upper, light regions. Formerly the door in the ceiling was open and the hole in the floor closed; today the tendency is the opposite. Today one rather reaches for the hells than for the heavens (*The Door in the Floor*, book title by John Irving). The hellish regions that can be reached through the "door in the floor" are vividly described in modern literature. For the heavenly regions reached through "the floor in the ceiling" one can go to much earlier literature. For example, St. Teresa of Ávila (1515-1582) describes a divine reality with many floors and many rooms. See A. Läpple 1988, pp. 185-192.

new study could have led to an amalgam of religion and psychology but rather marginalised religious thought and became a pseudo-religion.

The hubris of modern man is illustrated by Freud when he likened religion to a childhood neurosis, which he must overcome, arguing that "man cannot remain a child for ever." Man should rely on scientific rationalism and live heroically without illusions. He must rely on human knowing and, naked again as Adam and Eve in Eden, use psychotherapy as a fig leaf. This shows 'intellectual integrity' but he forgets that the human inner hunger is insatiable and needs more sustenance for a happy life than a fig leaf. In this respect he will always remain a child.

Thus, for Freud only the rational world counted. Having "said goodnight to sacred order"[113] and traditional faith, he was critical of anything that smacked of religion. He was, generally, satisfied with a secular material reality. But "when value is placed on externals, this always disturbs internally," says Chuang Tzu in the fourth century B.C.[114]

Freud sought scientific knowledge in the instincts, among them sexuality, and psychoanalysis was offered as the treatment of psychic aberration. That man needed spiritual values for a full life he seems never to have understood and he never acknowledged the 'oceanic feeling'. Jung, distancing himself from Freud, recognised psychic animation and the 'oceanic feeling.' Professing the necessity of a wider religious dimension, he escaped the paralysis of the one-sided Freudian approach.

Today, an increasing number of people are not satisfied with a world where religion is replaced by psychoanalysis. They turn to old beliefs or sell their souls to sects and charismatic leaders or even go to India to sit at the feet of a guru. They seek warm and spirited roads to "the still point of the turning world",[115] where peace reigns and where one feels beyond "name and form."

41. Activity – and Rest

Then, under the circumstances, perhaps four of the waking hours should be used for rest and leisurely speculation and contemplation over a lone-

---

[113] Freud quoted in M. Gundry 2006, p. 18.
[114] *Chuang Tzu*, ch. 19. Translation by J. R. Ware 1963.
[115] T. S. Eliot 1941.

ly glass and with a good cigar. Or one should perhaps spend them in siestas like the Spaniards or in a hammock like our food-gathering forefathers? Or like seamen resting their bones during the calm? Or reading a simple comic book on a grassy lawn? Or listening to music? Or reminiscing good old days? Or relishing short breaks? Or just feeling good? There must be better ways of leading a hectic life than navigating for sixteen hours through strain and anxiety. Every cell in the body suffers for it, and the soul exacts its revenge with tedium and frustration. One over-extends until one suffers a heart attack or experiences a nervous breakdown.

Overwork is one of the ills of modernity. One becomes trapped in a maze of routines until one can endure no more. Still one continues and often drives oneself to death. A popular word for this state is stress, a term less encountered in earlier ages. People are paying a price for over-extending, they do not live, they hardly exist. They are caught in quicksand that pulls them down and finally engulfs them.

We can make anything into a killing mania. In this age when we have the easy and comfortable life within reach or even in our hands, we drive exhaustingly for more. When we have started a project, there is excitement and soon one cannot wind down and relax. We tend to forget that proportion is required in all endeavours and situations. Whenever any undertaking runs amok, it is about time to stop and change the pace.

42. Memories

The personal storehouse of memories can be found, as it were, somewhere in the very middle along the seam joining mind and soul. Perhaps there is also in this respect a balance between what is inner and what is outer, on the brain side and on the mind side.[116]

Those who are familiar with their dreams notice time and again that the dreams come from both old and recent memories. They are coloured by the emotions of former experiences. The past is stored in the deep domain of the conscious-unconscious whole from where it floods up into the daylight and plays as essential a role as current happenings. The reliving of memories in our sleeping hours is as important as remembering

[116] It is argued that memories are "stored not in a single location but throughout the brain." J. Horgan 1999, pp. 20-21.

them in the waking hours. The memories relived in dreams constitute an unconscious mental depositary, which deserves to be taken seriously. We should strive to live so that good recollections accumulate and bad recollections are few. They cannot be changed. What we live and experience end up as our frozen past, as a storehouse of memories. Both in dream and awake we should cherish the good occurrences of former times.

The power of our memories should not be underestimated. Through them we bring our past into happy conjunction with the present and the future. We should never forget the good days we have lived. We can attempt to repress and perhaps forget the bad days and memories. This may prove to be difficult but we can make sure that the stressful days are buried under the recollections of the good days. A healthy psyche demands that we tend our memories carefully.

43. The Eternal and Memories

Memories lead into the eternal half of ourselves. If we do not feel so during the day, this is normal since we are immersed in the world of things and active life. But at night we cross the threshold to the eternal domain from where we have come and to where we shall return. Is not "Man's life between heaven and earth like the passing of a white colt glimpsed through a crack in the wall?"[117] These words originated in China and it could hardly be put more simply. This life is really little more than a crack in the massive Eternal. As Joseph Conrad puts it in his novel *The Mirror of the Sea*: "For what is the array of the strongest ropes, the tallest spars, and the stoutest canvas against the mighty breath of the infinite, but thistle stalks, cobwebs, and gossamer?" Even in broad daylight we cannot escape the fact that the temporal world is limited and that the Eternal beyond constitutes its vast other half. What temporal can indeed exist without its eternal other side, and vice versa? Unbalanced, nothing exists, and consequently the totality, the All, cannot be but balanced either. Looking to the right, looking to the left, we can see that everything comes full circle. Birth is matched by death, light by dark, good by evil. The Taoists apprehended this universal law when they wrote,

[117] *Chuang Tzu*, ch. 22. Translation by B. Watson 1968.

If there were no "that",
There would be no "this",
If there were no "this",
There would be nothing for all the winds to play on.[118]

How can we have any doubt about the Eternal? That side ought to be as lucid and logical to us as this side. It has been fashionable to 'doubt' since Descartes doubted everything except his own *cogito* and western man has practically managed to annihilate what is impossible to annihilate, the Eternal that envelops him and follows him as a shadow wherever he goes, from birth to death. It is his origin, beginning and end. Aware of this shadow his vision broadens and the material world is seen in a larger perspective.

44. Doubt West and Doubt East

Why is it that 'doubt' is so seldom heard in the East? Neither in India, nor in China, nor in Japan. If you mention doubt to an Indian, he may well wonder what you are talking about. He will probably tell you that his spiritual life is just as natural as his sensory life, as natural as the air he breathes. India possesses visions of the sacred which leave no room for doubt. No other civilization has focused for so long on finding clarity and wisdom. The situation in ancient China and Japan is similar. Why question or doubt something that constitutes what is, as a matter of fact, one's happiness? There is a great deal of debate on the form and content of various Asian religions such as Buddhism, Taoism, Shintoism, but doubt is hardly expressed.

Really, doubt is a western brain-child, and together with other western notions it has been exported and spread about the globe. On the occasion that young Japanese, for the most part city dwellers, express doubt about divine values, one can be sure that they belong to a later generation under the influence of the West.

Why did religious doubt develop in the West? Surely, it did not start with Descartes and a series of rationalists. Doubt, in fact, runs like a thread through Christianity from its cradle in Palestine and the Old Tes-

[118] Taoist poem, *Chuang Tzu*, ch. 2, expressing the nature of NATURE. *Measure for Measure*, says Shakespeare.

tament. The explanation must lie in the fact that the Eternal was reduced to an externalised God. Philosophy and religion were separated and the inherited world-view was shattered. The West began to focus on a world that was diminished to soulless dead matter and energy. When the Eternal was thus estranged, it could be loved, it could be hated – and it could be doubted.The same reduction of the Eternal never occurred in the East. The Spiritual was just the other side, inherent in all things. There was no reason to doubt the Eternal: It was found in what we see, hear, small, taste, touch and feel.[119]

To the intuitive life belong precognitions and premonitions, presentiments, forebodings and foreknowledge; further, coincidences and synchronicities, inspirations and clairvoyance, misgivings and warnings, signs and omens, the feeling of joy and well-being, the sense of light and harmony, the oceanic feeling, the Sixth Sense and 'gut feelings', wonders, hunches, all forms of 'inner knowledge'. One must be open to them. They give colour to personal existence.

If the Balance of all evolution and a cosmos governed by laws, discovered by Ptolemy, Newton, Einstein, Bohr, Heisenberg and others, are added, how can one doubt the Eternal either in the cosmic time or the personal life?[120] One can compare with the eastern vision of the whole, in which chaos always matches cosmos and comes first. The West lost this vision in the wake of Descartes and modern science – but it can be regained in a new insight of the contiguity of religion and science.[121]

Antoine de Saint-Exupéry (1900-1944) expressed pessimism about the development when he wrote late in life:

> For centuries humanity has been descending an immense staircase whose top is hidden in the clouds and whose lowest steps are lost in a dark abyss. We could

---

[119] "It is never numb and it speaks a different language than that of mathematics." W. R. Inge 1925, p. 382.

[120] When someone doubts the Eternal in the face of all these matters, one wonders whether there is not time for (new) glasses?

[121] D. Lack says, "Science has not accounted for morality, truth, beauty, individual responsibility or selfawareness ... in which a valid and central part of human experience lies outside science." D. Lack 1961, p. 114, in J. C. Eccles 1989, p. 235. "The ruined shrines of the goddess of reason are invaded by the rebel forces of *feeling*, will, imagination, and every obscure and primitive instinct." (Emphasis added). In W. R. Inge 1925, p. 360.

have ascended this staircase; instead we chose to descend it. Spiritual decay is terrible.[122]

This was written during the years of anguish of the Second World War. There was reason for pessimism in the face of war and totalitarian forces. One can, however, apply his vision of a staircase to the development since Descartes, leading step by step to the present materialism and intellectualism with more and more knowledge about less and less.

Today, in the West, intellectuals and students might declare God to be "dead" or "a sacred lie" (Nietzsche) and, in the East, Heaven might be repressed, but in people's hearts God and Heaven are neither dead nor forgotten – East or West.[123]

45. The longer Continuum

Man needs a longer continuum than the daily appetites. There is a need for the irrational in one form or another. Man needs his soul, his inner sanctuary, always amply sustained and in good keep. Modern man has become starved and homeless in proportion to the increase of material affluence. Material additions are permitted to compensate for spiritual emptiness.[124]

This situation can be seen in literature, film and television where all kinds of palliatives relieve the fundamental void within, that is, the missing essential dimension. Overemphasis on action, thrill and intoxication and other addictions can only be seen as attempts to fill an interior that is dreadfully vacuous. In contemporary dramas sex and romance coupled with the wild life, blood and murder rank high on the list of themes, while higher, absolute values are rarely distinguished. Man dances around the altar of prestige, profit, gain and wealth and can then sacrifice much and even commit murder. For a time he derives pleasure from

---

[122] Antoine de Saint-Exupéry, *Wartime Writings: 1939-1944*. Harcourt, 1986. "Pure intellect, detached from soul, is the death of man."

[123] Nietzsche might have declared God to be dead and replaced God "with a doctrine of vital energy as the source of everything human and divine but he never had any doubt that the conscious mind is the instrument of unconscious vitality." Quote from L. L. Whyte 1979, p. 175. Adapted.

[124] "Man ends up sacralising some aspect of the secular." D. Loy 2000, p. 155.

a boundless life but later the joy subsides into "the sorrowful emptiness inside the shell of luxury."[125] The eclipse of eternal values have, paradoxically, led to an obsession with death and posterity and, further, to an interest in success, wealth, fame, name and genealogy.

Man may live happily and comfortably as long as things move pleasantly, he is healthy and the social security net is intact under him. He might find quality of life – but not quality of death. In the end he will feel the transience and meaninglessness of profane living. It takes a strong person to face the void, when the world crumbles. The primary liaison of mind and soul is needed, before the final *Grenzsituation* can be confronted with magnanimity.

To strive for success is no sin as long as the efforts are inspired and in tune with the Will willing from the limitless depth of the soul. The efforts and successes should, however, not be attributed more importance than they deserve. Self-love can lead astray just as free market capitalism can be detrimental. Achievement can end up in a moral vacuum if not poised by good intent and altruism.[126]

Material objects cannot be appreciated without being harmonised within. The continuum must stretch from the interior world of the Eternal, forming the first half of the line, to the exterior world of reason and appearances, forming the second half. Poetry, song, art and music are necessary to even up prosaic life. Without an even share 'in there', what is 'out here' will always be one-sided and dreary. As it is, one must roam the inner half as much as the outer half. The inner half of man is as needed as the outer half – for a full and happy life.

46. The Time Continuum

Once the basic inner-outer continuum is in order, one can turn to other continua that are also necessary for the fullness of life. The three modes of time in the midst of everyday existence come next. One certainly exists in the 'now', the brief hour on earth but "Le présent est chargé du passé, et gros de l'avenir" (Leibniz)[127] and "Das Heute geht gespeist durch das

[125] Ford Madox Ford, *The Good Soldier*. The sad end of a sad story.
[126] C. Wilson 1966, p. 127.
[127] Leibniz is quoted in E. Cassirer 1944, p. 50. "The present is charged with the past

Gestern in das Morgen." (Brecht).[128] On one side of the present one has the past and on the other the future, and these three 'times' form a cycle that enriches the 'interior silence'.[129]

Past, present and future form a fundamental three-dimensional unity. The present is influenced by what has been, and all that is to come cannot be considered without the cushion of the past. One dwells in the Eternal 'now', this 'atom of eternity', about which S. Kierkegaard writes in passionate terms: "life must be lived forwards – and be understood backwards." We must allow present, past and future to blend and the ever-fleeting present to swallow the past! "Life is a continuum of 'nows' in which future is yet to come."[130] Like the Buddhist "one must not repent of the past, nor brood over the future but live in the present."[131] It is the now that counts. As Jakob Böhme writes,

> He to whom time is the same as eternity
> And eternity the same as time
> Is free from all contention.[132]

How 'the atom of eternity' differs from the past and the future! It is the brief sojourn on earth in which eternity and temporality meet and when the future crystallises and becomes the past. It surpasses the relativity of the sensible world as choices are made relating to absolute life and its grand design. The past and the future intertwine with the pre-eminent present, separated from each other "by the elusive and ever-fleeting wall of the now."[133] It is common to forget the past, and disregard the future, when, in this throwaway age, one lives in a "permanent present", moving from place to place and up and down the social ladder. But as W. Churchill said, "The longer you look backward, the further you can look forward."

> It is not so that we have so little time, but that we waste so much of it. (Seneca)
> Every passing moment is a treasure, in joy as in adversity. (M. Ricard)

---

and filled with the future."

[128] Bertolt Brecht (1898-1956): "Today, fed by the yesterday, goes into the morrow."

[129] T. S. Eliot 1941: "Time present and time past are both present in time future, and time future is contained in time past."

[130] Time is part of the sacredness of creation. See N. M. Wildiers 1968, p. 55.

[131] Buddha's words quoted in D. Loy 2000, p. 47.

[132] Böhme quoted in D. Loy 2000, p. 39.

[133] N. M. Wildiers 1968, p. 55.

In Japan the present contains the past. People keep memories and memorabilia as part of life! It is a Japanese virtue to preserve old things among new things. In China, too, behind the Communist facade, one can perceive the ancient dimension. When China settles down as one of the great nations of the world, it will hark back to its past, not merely labelling it "feudal" but be proud of its great ancient roots. The same respect for the past is at the root of the cultivation of the "native village." Japanese honour their *furusato*, and return there regularly. This is part of ancestral religion. Even during the Cultural Revolution the Chinese sent the ashes of their dead to be buried in their native village.

47. Eternal Time and Cosmic Time

Today, few people embrace spontaneous and intuitive life. People rush through time. For most people past and present blend into each other, and the future is, for the most part, taken for granted. Burials turn into routine affairs, and the dead are soon forgotten – even before they are buried. Time has become the permanent present, a concrete and living reality with an irreversible onward rush.

The welfare state in a number of countries deprives individuals of worries about the future. A false sense of security makes them even turn their back on the shadow of death. 'Clock time' or 'historical time' becomes the only 'time', and if it were not for the intermittent existential shocks, people would be little more than 'identical castings off an assembly line.' Historical times reigns and eternal time is ignored.

There is the Eternal Time at a higher level than the physical time. The latter is the historical time that can be subdivided into years, days and hours. It is nature in flux and change.

In ancient Greece and in the East time was eternal and so it was in the West until the Middle Ages. Likewise, Christ saw time in an eternal light. Man's time was much like the entelechial time in nature where every moment is both now and eternal, as professed by Aristotle.[134, 135]

---

[134] Aristotle's entelechy (*entelecheia*) is the principle of nature, unconscious and holistic, and close to the Neo-Confucian *li* principle in *chi* matter-energy. "A purposiveness runs through all nature, sleeping in the stone, dreaming in the flower, and partially awake and conscious in man." W. R. Inge 1925, p. 367.

[135] "Time disappears with the things," says A. Einstein.

48. Dreams and Expectations

A sense of expectation prepares the ground for moments to come and is a thrill in itself. "At no time are we ever in such complete possession of a journey, down to its last nook and cranny, as when we are busy with preparations for it."[136] An object is most-prized and appreciated when steeped in anticipation. Intuition can guide us to paths of our very own. Who can explain signals to the conscious making people to set goals in life? Are they dreams – or flashes of intuition and vision – that make them stretch out their arms and behave in certain ways? Throughout the continuous stream of instants, a dialectical process becomes recognised, starting out with a vision about the future and ending as a recollection. The rocket passes from anticipation to anticipation, all ending up as memories. Dreams and visions speak to man from the hidden reaches of the inner. He must be open to the Whole and receptive to the signals. As Arthur Rimbaud says, "The symphony stirs in the depths or comes on the scene at a leap."[137]

There are, of course, wishful dreams – moments of fantasy and foresight – that never actually materialise. 'The idle daydreams' should, however, not be underestimated – nuggets of gold are found among them. The dreaming, whether awake or asleep, is important. The dreams mirror what is sleeping in the soul. They occur for a reason, whether they are of an everyday routine or of a new and life-changing kind. They add value and colour to a person's life and help him to thrive and grow.

Like all life they require the dimension of *sub specie aeternitatis* ("under the light of eternity") in order to be complete. Whether one admits it or not, one is always in the shadow of infinity, and one had better befriend the Eternal during the short span on earth. This can be done in thousands of ways, as witnessed in the religions around the globe.[138]

The visions and anticipations should be lived *sub specie aeternitatis*, and weighed and measured sensibly. Dreams can turn into nightmares if they do not occur to the well-balanced and discriminating mind and soul. Today when the whole world has opened up and temptations are

---

[136] Y. Mishima 1958, p. 91.
[137] A. Rimbaud is quoted in L. L. Whyte 1979, p. 172.
[138] D. A. Graham 1971, p. 6 *et passim*.

advertised in rosy colours, it is up to the individual to screen what is served and choose what is deeply felt as the right thing. In this manner many allurements will be avoided, one keeps to the minimum and it will have the fulfilling quality that satisfies mind and heart. One must know one's measure and live accordingly.

Following one's inspiration and true measure, one adds eternity to daily life. One perceives then that the mysterious Chance and the enigmatic Coincidentia will intervene on one's behalf. The joy of inner consciousness will have true ring. This is to allow the Timeless and Eternal to play a significant part in our affairs. It presents the incessant pearls of thrilling moments – and that hilarious sensation of living *sub specie aeternitatis*.

49. The Mind and the Body

Complicated is the soul-heart-mind-body continuum whose conjunction and equilibrium is essential for a happy life. While the body connects with the world, the heart aligns with the soul.[139] Man has the complex span of soul, heart, mind and body in a single weave. He is spiritual, emotional, moral and intellectual in one sweep. The heart and mind are in the middle, the pivot of the intuitive soul and the cognitive intellect. A gap has opened between heart and mind in western thought, a gap that never existed in the East. In China and Japan, for example, the term *shin* 心 (Jap. *kokoro*), best translated as 'heart-mind', comprises both

[139] "Since materialist solutions fail to account for our experienced uniqueness, I am constrained to attribute the uniqueness of the Self or Soul to a supernatural spiritual creation. To give the explanation in theological terms: each Soul is a new Divine creation which is implanted into the growing foetus at some time between conception and birth. It is the certainty of the inner core of unique individuality that necessitates the 'Divine creation'. ... No other explanation is tenable; neither the genetic uniqueness with its fantastically impossible lottery, nor then environmental differences which do not *determine* one's uniqueness, but merely modify it. ... This reinforces our belief in the human Soul and its miraculous origin in a Divine creation. There is recognition not only of the Transcendent God, the Creator of the Cosmos, the god in which Einstein believed, but also of the loving God to whom we owe our being. ... It is a miracle for ever beyond science." J. C. Eccles 1989, pp. 236-237.

feeling (heart) and knowing (mind) with emphasis on the heart. In the West the heart with its sentiments has become separated from the mind and the senses. They have divided and the emphasis is placed on the mind. This has given rise to Western rationalism, empiricism, naturalism, scienticism and other isms whereas spiritual happenings are referred to as mysticism and occultism. In thought and literature there has been a shift of emphasis from the cognitive toward the unconscious aspects of reality. Still, the attempts have often tended to remain 'a preoccupation with the unconscious' on the rational side of things – only.[140]

Outward follows the body with its instinctual energies, hunger, aggression, power and sex, of which the sex urge is possibly the strongest. Sex, "the great dark overabundance", "the great underground canal of hidden sexual passion"... "that storms day and night like a gale through the metropolis"[141] is the psychic energy that runs deeply through the veins of body and mind and more often than not plays havoc with its host. It is "the most precious spark of Nature's fire" (Jefferson). Man must coexist with it and bring it into harmony with other urges. It has played as significant a role in history, as has the lust of wealth and power and has roused man to action as much as to love and hatred.

> Eroticism pervades our culture and upbringing and provides the pictures that fill the background of our lives; our desire for 'escape,' which a mechanical boredom exacerbates. ... We look upon passion as a transfiguring force, something beyond pain and delight, an ardent beatitude.[142]

All human urges require handling with care. They demand outlets in their right proportions, be levelled and sublimated in the balanced individual; if not, the incurred imbalance can ultimately affect the person in his entirety.

50. The Good Word and Deed at the Right Time

Acts of kindness serve to create affinity and remove barriers – even mountains – provided they originate from a sincere mind. A smile can open a hundred doors. Good deeds can achieve the same. Essentially,

140 See L. L. Whyte 1979, p. 127ff.
141 Y. Mishima 1973.
142 D. de Rougemont 1956, p. 15, quoted in D. Loy 2000, pp. 139-140.

neither kindness nor good deeds should be performed in excess. They should be conferred according to context and circumstance. Neither the busybodies nor the do-gooders are met with approval. Any form of assistance must be afforded spontaneously as though it never happened. Kind words must be delivered with a personal touch rendering the person speaking almost non-existent. Word or deed proffered superficially and without sincerity and empathy need not be said or done at all.

Words can but express a mere semblance of the inexpressible, the silent language deep within us. Typically, language is used, in terms of analogy, for things beyond name and form and space and time. Such analogies have at times gone too far, and man's fabulation has strayed. For our purpose it is of importance, however, that such analogies have been drawn east, west, north and south to describe the same enlightenment.

One cannot overlook that Indians, Japanese, Hebrews and Greeks along with many others shared the same experience and expressed it in ever new ways. This provides man with occurrences of illumination from all corners of the globe and with a wealth of rich comparative materials that can be to his advantage. Hence it can be concluded that the revelation has been described whenever man was able to verbalise it and that, as a result, he can turn to numerous written sources for sustenance. Browsing through this literature, one will come upon new analogies and one will realise that others attained the same inward fulfilment – in just a different light. Turning to Lao Tzu's *Tao-Te-Ching* or to the Indian *Bhagavad-Gita*, readers reap as much sustenance for the soul as when reading the Bible. Similarly myths and legends, passed down throughout the ages all over the world and registered by scholars of anthropology, sociology and other disciplines, provide material with a similar overall comprehension. In the end all traditions reveal the inner freedom, the joy in living, – the 'innerism' – espoused in this work. Inner and outer seem to be a dualism, but they are rather "an explicit duality expressing an implicit unity."[143]

One can have the same moments of lucidity when studying the Bible in a new language. Passages so familiar that they lose their weight in one's own language and one is untouched by them, appear fresh and novel, revealing the old truths shrouded in new garb.

---

[143] A. W. Watts 1975, p. 26, in his discussion of *yin* and *yang*.

To assure success in spiritual endeavour it is essential to shake off habits of worldly vanity. As long as belief in one religion or prophet remains the foundation of thought and wisdom, claiming infallible cognition of truth, it remains impossible to oust religious intolerance. The openness and willingness to accept other creeds remains a true sign of a person who leads an inspired life. He generously accepts what others have perceived and finds verification in other traditions. He allows no one to have a monopoly of the divine truth.[144]

51. Language and Words

As human beings we have acquired the skill of language, this "most momentous and mysterious product of the "human mind," [145] but it is an unsatisfactory tool for expressing and interpreting matters. Careless use of language can cause misunderstandings – and words can run out of steam! Words must, however, be used and language is our foremost means to translate what is experienced. When language is correctly employed as a vehicle of the human mind and enhanced with images and metaphors, it serves also as a means of memorizing and an aid to self-realization. We utilise concepts and terms as much when we talk to ourselves as when communicating with others. It is said that you talk as well as laugh inwardly. Hence we can conclude that though words are merely symbols, they serve us well. They can express truth and what is felt "metaphorically, allegorically, symbolically, figuratively, analogically as well as literally."[146]

Our inside can also address us. There is such a thing as soul conversation. When we read about conversations with gods and angels that occur in practically all religions, can we not deduce that it refers to such intercourse? As St. John wrote, "Words can be spirit and they can be life."

---

[144] "Same in art, unique in part – as a unique self-conscious being, in each self." J. C. Eccles 1989, p. 236.

[145] S. K. Langer 1956, p. 94. "Everything which is not speakable thought, is feeling." And "at best, human thought is but a tiny, grammar-bound island, in the midst of a sea of feeling." *Ibid.* pp. 81-82.

[146] L. Wieseltier, in review of D. C. Dennet 2006, p. 114.

Further, words can remind us of events half forgotten and evoke tender feelings that include pleasure and joy and harmony with their glow.

As we face up to life, we should abide by intuitive harmony, and be content with the private joy of inner consciousness without words. "Only in joy can the human being awaken and fulfil itself until free from all lack, it matures to the divine."[147]

The mere fact of living ought to suffice. What we need in our day and age are the lived examples. We should follow *Zen* experience in which clarity follows upon introspection – without words. Inner knowing goes beyond verbal communication. Most *Zen* sects leave the written word aside and require nothing but *satori* enlightenment. How ironic, then, that there has been more written about *Zen* than about Buddhism otherwise!

52. Knowledge and Wisdom

For presumably as long as man has existed on this planet, beliefs and creeds have matched cognition and science. Only in recent centuries the emphasis has been placed on the intellect and sensual cognition. Science and faith have been fenced off from each other by a seemingly impenetrable barrier. Knowledge of things has come to outdistance the knowledge of man. It is said by Bacon that "Pure intellect, detached from soul, is the death of man." [148]

Knowledge always served wisdom, and it was never cast adrift from intuition to fend for itself. This was true in all parts of the world, not merely in Europe. To seek knowledge just for the sake of knowledge and not for the sake of wisdom has been the trend since the Renaissance (ca. 1500-1620) and is a Western phenomenon that has spread and is about to conquer the world more successfully than any religion.

In India and Japan, however, this schism is not conspicuous in spite of the advances of science and technology. Subjective stillness and objective activity form a continuum and remain intact also in our day. Advances in positivistic knowledge have not resulted in the within of man being

---

[147] Martin Buber (1878-1965), in *Tales of Rabbi Nachman.*

[148] Bacon also said that, "A little knowledge often estranges men from religion, a deeper knowledge brings them back again."

cast aside. In our technical world it is more important than ever to keep the inner open to balance an outer world that threatens to become ever more cold and inhuman. For millions of years man's inner and outer formed a continuum in the fields of the infinite. Now the outward horizons are expanding while the inward vistas are receding.[149] The wisdom that said, "empiric in deed and holistic in creed", is gone.

53. Today's Intellectualism

The emphasis on the human condition has rendered the western thinker "a habitual lier", as Jung puts it. For his part Eric Hoffer (1902-1983) expressed the opinion that education is not necessarily for the better. He visualised a country governed by common-sense men and women instilled with sound practical knowledge rather than long education. He once voiced the idea that dock workers from San Francisco would do better in Washington than over-educated Harvard graduates from well-off families without experience of ordinary working life.

The intellectuals themselves, in the vanguard of modernity, have erred into ever new 'isms' that are complex and above the horizons of the majority of people. They are the professors of philosophy, and their messages are directed exclusively to the initiated within the academic milieu – and are hardly even acknowledged among them. Their thought is generally inflated with new vocabulary requiring explanation. Only professional cliques are expected to read them. The result has been that most people interested in their thought turn to secondary sources where messages are presented in the concise form that they could have been given originally.

Modern thinkers often create a cold academic atmosphere anchored in new worldly constructs. If they are not to be dubbed liers, as Jung suggested, they are 'charlatans' who fool the world. Eric Hoffer was right. Education is not necessarily for the better; it can alienate man as much as further him.

---

149 We are "approaching scientific ability to control men's thought with precision." When Winston Churchill (1874-1965) heard this chilling news, he replied that he would "be very happy to be dead before that happens." One tends to agree with him. See J. W. Krutch 1953, pp. 44-45.

54. Religion versus Science and Atheism

What most modern thinkers have in common is the repudiation of God and the divine and the emphasis on the physical-chemical material realm.

Already Pierre-Simon Marquis de Laplace (1749-1827) could tell Napoleon that "God was no longer a necessary hypothesis in celestial mechanics" and Auguste Comte (1798-1857) recommended that society should be worshipped instead of God. In the mid-twentieth century, secular ideologues like Ambrose Bierce (1842-1914) said that "Christianity was an antiquated superstition with no place in the modern world"[150] and Julian Huxley (1887-1975) stated that "to-day God is becoming an erroneous hypothesis in all aspects of reality, including man's life."[151] The scholar Charles Darwin (1809-1882) (*Origin of Species*, 1859) became the "Darwinist" believer in later works such as *The Descent of Man* (1871). In these works and in polemical writings by Darwin's supporters[152]the war between science and religion was declared. The conflict between science and religion is thus of a recent date. Now "Man had to choose between being on the side of the apes or on the side of the angels."[153] The order of religious and civil life tipped in a secular direction, when Naturalism was accepted by a large segment of the intelligentsia. In this 'post-Christian' age metaphysics became a word of abuse as warfare was raging between science and religion.[154] Ernst Haeckel (1834-1919) announced "a new religion for the new man – on the sure ground of modern science, a religion that overcomes all previous religions."[155] Today it is discussed how the mind and the brain depend on each other. The brain is a body organ composed of cells but the mind is not. The intricate connection between the two has yet to be established.[156] It is said

---

[150] Ambrose Bierce, quoted in *The Economist*, December 23, 2006, p. 81.

[151] J. Huxley 1957, p. 246.

[152] First among them, Thomas Henry Huxley.

[153] Social idealism and mechanical progress have replaced religion.

[154] The science of Darwin has been exchanged for the religion of Darwin. As L. van der Post says: "This rift between the religions and the scientific needs of man has been widening and deepening over the last century and has, plainly, cloven his mind in two." See also M. Gundry 2006, pp. 53-54.

[155] E. Haeckel is quoted in M. Nagy 1991, p. 244.

[156] J. C. Eccles and D. N. Robinson 1984, pp. 66-68, and W. H. Thorpe 1961, p. 22 and

that religion will disappear with ever-greater scientific understanding and psychology hardening into science.[157]

It should be noticed, however, that the materialistic domination is by no means total. Even in the West it is mostly limited to intellectual circles. Science has not managed to suppress man's inherent religious inclination. Among common people the 'free-thinker' and atheist are still rare. In the United States more than 90% of the population profess to believe in a personal God and recent investigations show that a majority in Europe believe in God, for example, 60% of the population in Sweden and 55% in Germany.

"In fact", as Karen Armstrong writes, "beyond Western Europe, Canada and a few other countries, religion maintains a growing global presence. A 44-nation survey by the Washington-based 'Pew Forum on Religion & Public Life' found that 8 in 10 Africans consider religion as very important personally, a figure rivaled or exceeded in the Middle East, most of Asia and every Latin American country except Argentina. Significantly, the United States stands virtually alone among the world's wealthiest nations in the importance its people place on religion in both their private lives and the public sphere."... "Religiosity is not dead but good religion is in danger of being engulfed by bad religion. Bad religion is the suffocation of the sacred by dogma, by artificial rules; it stifles the individual's search for the absolute truth beyond visible appearances, often by investing worldly values in what is ultimately sacred. As Jung noted, 'so much religious practice seems designed precisely to prevent people from having an experience beyond existence. Good religion is the embrace of compassion and confrontation with the "other", which is the kernel of the teachings of all the great traditions. Compassion is the key to religion, the key to spirituality.' "[158]

---

p. 28. A. Damasio says, "The brain's body-furnished, body-minded mind is a servant of the whole body." (A. Damasio 2003, p. 207) J. Horgan says, "Basically the brain is unconscious." (J. Horgan 1999, p. 30) "What operations of the human brain-mind admit exact analysis?" L. L. Whyte 1979, p. 181.

[157] But "the psyche has a 'religious function' that will remain a part of human reality indefinitely, quite apart from the fate of the traditional Western religions." M. Gundry 2006, with reference to Jung, p. 67. In any case, brain and mind must cooperate for man to be alive.

[158] K. Armstrong 2005b, pp. 52-53: "After India the United States is probably the most religious nation in today's world."

Perhaps, as Teilhard de Chardin (1881-1955) says, "a new, until now unprecedented, form of religion (a religion that no one has yet been able to visualise or describe ...) is germinating in the heart of man today ... ."[159] It is obvious that "any theory that finds room for mind and spirit ... must be far nearer to the religious view of reality than the Naturalism of the last century."[160]

55. The Cartesian Wall

In both Egyptian and Babylonian thought chaos preceded cosmos. This world was a means to prepare for another. The pyramids are the most visible memory of this thinking. Similarly in the East the beginning and emphasis of thought lay on the 'other side'. In China the cosmic order, the Way, the *Tao*, was considered to be the essence and the law of all things. It is the Eternal of Chinese philosophies and religions. The same outlook can, *mutatis mutandis*, be found in Japanese and eastern thought generally.

The Greeks began early to take an interest in cosmic matters. They focused upon the living world and the laws of nature under the umbrella of a Heaven where Zeus was the Lord and where Destiny reigned even over the gods. Man's efforts were invariably linked to religion, and nature and gods were never divided.

The Christian era represent no alteration. God was never denied and every new discovery was proclaimed in his name and considered a piece of his marvellous Creation. In the medieval centuries the Christian synthesis[161] reached its climax with St. Thomas Aquinas (1225-1274). A universe was imagined in which nature served man and mankind served God. This Christian age continued during the transition to the modern period via the Renaissance and the great scientific discoveries of the sixteenth and seventeenth centuries. Descartes, Copernicus, Kepler, New-

[159] T. de Chardin quoted in N. M. Wildiers 1968, p. 114. T. A. Metzger (1977, p. 231) is more pessimistic when he says that a religious 'breakthrough' does not seem to be on the horizon."

[160] W. R. Inge 1925, p. 373.

[161] "The rational theology of scholasticism with only one set of standards." M. Nagy 1991, p. 50.

ton and other leading scientists never forgot their being God's servants and their revelations were declared to be only 'pebbles on the shore of an infinite ocean.' Their scientific successes meant no transformation of their overall medieval view of life. The tension between 'how to go to Heaven' and 'how the Heavens go' did not exist. Bacon and Montaigne (1533-1592) evince no conflict between the two. Interest turned, however, in the favour of the latter, the upshot being a reduced God, a 'god of the gaps' "inhabiting whatever dark corners science had not yet brought to rational light."[162] The emphasis turned from contemplation to the study of the material world. "The nineteenth century developed an extremely rigid frame for natural science which formed not only science but also the general outlook of the great masses of people."[163] In our day, the universe has moved from the "strict Newtonian laws or regular movements of 'clocks' to the laws of chance or statistical probability, the random movements of 'clouds' whose configurations in any individual instance cannot even theoretically be predicted."[164]

Actually, it was only in the West, and after the French Enlightenment in the eighteenth century, that, in Whitehead's words, "science saddled religion."[165] None of the early scientific breakthroughs seriously affected religion. "Only in the nineteenth century, after Darwin, was the supposed irreconcilability between 'God' and 'science' elevated to the status of cultural myth."[166] Rational consciousness was cultivated and religion was equated with ignorance and superstition.[167] This did not happen in the East or in the Islamic world.

Still, the Enlightenment was a blessing for mankind. It was the *Aufklärung* that was needed to bring about the modern world, the end product being secular democracy and liberal economy. And a vigilant *Aufklärung* – and a Voltaire (1694-1778) – are relevant in every age, consid-

---

[162] Kenneth L. Woodward quoted in *Newsweek*, July 27, 1998, p. 50, "How the Heavens Go."

[163] W. Heisenberg 1959, pp.168-169.

[164] K. L. Woodward, quoted in R. H. Torrance 1994, p. 276. Cf., F. Herneck 1963, pp. 51-57.

[165] A. N. Whitehead 1925, p. 36.

[166] K. L. Woodward, *ibid.*

[167] C. G. Jung laments that "Christian tenets have lost their authority and their psychological justification."

ering how delusional man tends to be. As T. Jefferson (1743-1826) said, "eternal vigilance is the price of liberty."[168]

56. Inspiration and Science

Scientific work must be related to inspiration. Directly or indirectly all insights are immediate and intuitive. Intuition comes first and knowledge follows. It is essential that we do not disregard this fact in the hubris of progress as we penetrate the galaxies and the subatomic particles, using the telescope, the microscope and other instruments.

In earlier times, East and West, learning was for the sake of WISDOM. Today, on the other hand, the scientist proudly states that it is knowledge for the sake of knowledge! Strindberg wrote with disdain about the scientist's "knappologi"[169] and Goethe's Faust expressed his disillusionment with the futility of amassed learning which hits a wall beyond which it cannot go. Only "dein Sinn ist zu, dein Herz ist TOT!" sighs Faust. He has studied at all faculties – philosophy, medicine, law, theology – but "feels no wiser than before."[170] It dawns on him that "The tree of knowledge is not that of life." He despairs and is ready to commit suicide when the inner in the shape of Christianity intervenes and circumstances change.

We lose the grasp of the Whole when we concentrate overly on its patterns. We must comprehend the Whole first, then, afterwards, take an interest in its parts. By looking too closely at the parts we may lose sight of the Whole altogether. [171]

There are panoramas inwards, stretching far beyond the regions of sensation and cyberspace. There is an inner science which is equally important as outer science. Freud, Adler, Jung and others have endeavoured to map this mental world. In the wake of their research things have come to light not conceived of a few generations ago. Their conclusion is that life transcends physics, chemistry and mathematics.

---

[168] Also ascribed to Wendell Phillips (1852); quoted in D. C. Dennet 2006, p. 334.
[169] "Pedantic systematization of worthless facts." Swedish term introduced by August Strindberg (1849-1912).
[170] Goethe's Faust, 1st act. He recognises that all is transitory and only a symbol.
[171] M. Polanyi 1997, p. 318.

We shall not let modern presumptions make us think that the affinity with the great totality is no longer needed. 'The soul's eye' and intuition are as necessary today as in yonder days.[172] Scientific discoveries and the religious function should walk peacefully together, hand in hand.[173] The inner vistas cannot be described consciously, but this does not mean that they are not known in myths, legends and allegories. History reveals the interplay of unconscious and conscious processes. It discloses how little man's rational mind was in control of things. Since the seventeenth century, however, "science calls the tune, and religion dances to its music."[174] Or as R. W. Emerson put it, "things are in the saddle and ride mankind."[175]

57. The Multi-dimensional Life

To lead a full life we need dimensions that add to our animal existence, give it wings, make it human. One-dimensional life is not enough for lasting peace, nor is two-dimensional or three-dimensional life. There are more dimensions required that extend beyond the cosmic dimensions. Man shall allow for a genuine life to have as many qualities as we expect to find in a novel that will be read long after it was first published. It must be well written, have literary style, mixing the poetic with the prosaic, mingling sincerity with humour, remoteness with nearness, Heaven with Earth, and other aspects discovered by the author in and through himself, elements that add up to a true author. When it is merely technically perfect, the novel will not last long, no matter how well formulated it is. The same can be said of an individual's life. If the life does not embrace the qualities of a rich psyche, it will remain void and dry as "graves which men walk over without being aware of them."[176]

People need challenges. People need to take risks. They must accept chances. Life is full of them and presents aha-experiences when the mind is open to them. To live this manifest life might mean mistakes and

---

[172] H. J. Eysenck 1952, p. 159.
[173] E. T. Martin 1952, p. 234.
[174] K. R. Miller 1999, p. 288.
[175] Emerson is quoted in W. Durant 1953, p. 377.
[176] *Luke*, 11: 44.

suffering hardships. As Mark Twain (1835-1910) said, however, "we must have the courage to face fear but not to succumb to fear." And remember the Chinese wisdom that says, "Man is the helpless thing of chance" (*I Ching*). The greatest risk is not to take risks![177]

Per aspera ad astra, "through difficulties to the stars", is an old Roman saying expressing that the accomplished man is the result of the trials of life. That health needs difficulties is often overlooked in our overprotected modern societies. People demand safety nets before they step out on the tightrope – life insurance before they venture venture.[178] The Chinese and Japanese asserted the *per aspera ad astra* thinking with the concept *nan-i k'un-chiung* 難儀困窮 (Jap. *nangi-konkyû*), [achievement through] difficulties and hardships.

58. The Minimal Life

At the end of the day one is left with little time for more than things that enrich and widen the scope of human life. Especially in an age when people are flooded relentlessly with material goods that glitter enticingly and beckon to be taken in possession, it is necessary to steel oneself against temptation and ask whether this or that is needed on top of other belongings. Having confronted the temptation, one will grasp the fact that, more often than not, a new item is false gold that only glimmers and is of no value. The soul is lost in unnecessary possessions. Overconsumption makes people vacuous.

Collecting possessions, people could opt to follow criteria that bestow extra value and dimension on each object. They could collect things that remind the beholder of a particular event or person. They could see to it that each article in their possession is a gift, thus radiating the memory of a loved person or a special occasion. Any true object should thus have the extra worth that gives meaning and contentment. Life actually be-

---

[177] F. Johansson 2004, p. 191.

[178] The Chinese philosopher Mencius expressed the *aspera ad astra* concept in the following manner: "When Heaven is about to confer a great office on any man, it first exercises his mind with suffering, and his sinews and bones with toil. It exposes his body to hunger and subjects to extreme poverty. These measures stimulate his mind and harden his nature. *Mêng Tzu* VI: 1, 2 and 15: 2.

comes richer the fewer the objects are and when only the articles are acquired which give lustre to a person's existence and environment. With a minimum of things, people are happier.

Much travel in our day of boundless opportunities is often only for the sake of travelling. The nurture and gain that was once part and parcel of pilgrimages and journeys has been relegated to the shelves of a curiosity shop. Travel was only for the fewest of the few not many years ago. The jet-age ascended upon mankind with a burst of innovative activity and became another object which makes man, literally, run away from himself. Travel in its right proportion and for the right purpose can be a balsam to the soul and enrich life as a whole. Excessive travel, on the other hand, narrows the mind.

It is also worth mentioning a person's circle of friends and acquaintances. Also in this respect there is need for limitation. Friendship implies few friends rather than many. An excess of intimates will prove superfluous. He is a happy man who has the absolute minimum of people about himself. The rare people who bring dimensions to personal life and friendship that lasts a lifetime are enough.

Contentment with little makes a rich life. Beauty is to be found in less not more. Then, paradoxically, one will be amazed at the beauty of it all. "Things lead a man astray. Be a master of things rather than mastered by things," says a Chinese philosopher.[179] Meister Eckhart says: "There where clinging to things end, is where God begins to be."[180]

59. The Simple Life

One further continuum that induces rapport is the potent mix of civic life with elements of primitivism and simplicity.

It is essential to prevent the overcivilised modes of modernization and secularisation to take over all aspects of life. This is the tendency in the western purportedly progressive countries. The sterile products thereof can be viewed walking and moving along streets. Modernism needs tempering and spicing and we must hark back to the old-fashioned

---

[179] Hsün Tzu (ca. 320-245 B.C.), quoted in D. J. Munro 1969, p. 89.

[180] In M. Fox 1983, p. 54.

ways, which we lived for millions of years before present-day civilization.

The adding of spice can be done in many ways. One way is to take one day off each week when one lives a more natural life without all the commodities which one is normally engulfed by. One can be a little behind the trends of the times and keep what is old and decripit. One can potter about in one's garden, one can let one's beard grow on Sundays; one can forget to wash oneself one day a week. One can go out in true nature during weekends and smell a flower under a tree like Ferdinando, pondering nothing in particular. Truth is found among the foliage of a tree and in the scent of the grass.

To keep in regular touch with those who are less fortunate amongst us gives perspective to life. The poor, the aged, the lonely, the homeless, the crippled, the handicapped and the weak are among us, and will remain there no matter what social programme. Often to our surprise, they are more well-adjusted than men of fortune and wealth.[181] It is important for the privileged to maintain close and healthy relations with the underprivileged, just as the same can be said of the underprivileged maintaining healthy relations with the privileged.

All relationships must just be authentic and classless. If they do not carry the ring of empathy, they might as well not take place at all. Many social ills would be alleviated if we made friends with the unlike as with the like. Retaining childish openness is a way to be in touch with others. Strange as it might seem, clumsiness appears endearing. One can be playful and warm, it is liked. One can crack a joke, feign ignorance, it reaches people as much as intelligent utterances.

60. The Old and the Young

There is also a balance to be struck between the old and the young. Today a chasm has opened up between the generations, and three generations rarely live together under the same roof. Until a few generations ago, through the millennia, the young, the middle-aged and the old co-

[181] As G. Hardin says in *Nature and Man's Fate* (1958, p. 221): "The outcast, the impoverished, and the lonely man sometimes has an immense advantage over the accepted 'well-adjusted' man of wealth." Cf. *Luke*, 18: 24.

habited, mostly in a single room, hut, cave or tent. They lived together and they died together. This resulted in security throughout their lives, as they established affinities and sympathies with each other. This sense of fellowship vanishes in our advanced societies. The old lead their separate lives, often lonely and forgotten in their sunset years. Children have their private rooms, and leave home as soon as age allows it.

We have lost our grasp on the fundamental family, and it must be recovered. Regaining touch with the generations will add significance to the lives of the young, as well as providing solace to the old, as they approach their final hour. And what of the middle-aged? They are placed in the middle, and the burden lies on their shoulders for seniors and juniors alike. This responsibility gives meaning to their lives. Allowing the welfare state to take care of things which belong to people naturally impoverishes the human existence. Why work and toil through the best years if it is not for one's family? In many cultures one still lives in a wider 'familism' which includes generations bygone and generations to come.

61. Dionysian versus Apollonian

Temperament is another continuum leading from the young to the old. The young are characterised by the Dionysian spirit, making them exuberantly energetic and crying for new lands to conquer. It is the age of rapture and ecstasy. Things lie open and promising and death is rarely considered, seeming so removed. This is the reason why the young go to war – and die.[182]

Over the years human beings acquire the Apollonian disposition, they perceive things more through reason, law and order, and less through sentiment. In mature age, when the final hour is closing in, things are seen in darker colours and one is no more ready to stake all on one game. One avoids the tightrope and one prefers to sit where it is comfortable.

They are a beauty of opposites, the young and the old, as they form a pair that match each other. In-between are the middle-aged with an eye

---

[182] This passage is influenced by F. Nietzsche. See K. F. Reinhardt 1952, pp. 69-70.

in either direction, still Dionysian enough for occasional excitement and yet old enough to wish for an Appolonian order of life. It is their task to be the pivot and stretch out one hand to the young staving off their worst excesses and at the same time reach out to the old who have lost the vigour of their youth but still wish to be involved and not by-passed.

It should not be disregarded that some are born more Dionysian and others more Apollonian. Not only are they born so, but they stay so throughout life, understandably mellowing with advanced years and physical ailments. Churchill was certainly full of Dionysos through his entire life, and Chamberlain was without doubt as orderly as a child as he was later as a statesman.

When born with a Dionisian temperament one is of course more vulnerable than someone born with an Apollonian temper. Chamberlain sits where he sits and hurts no one – and no one harms him; Churchill is always on the move, and he leaves a wake behind him – and remains vulnerable. Thus human beings form a mosaic ranging from the passionate to the inert.

62. Measure and Proportion

No mania shall be allowed the upper hand in life's equilibrium. No one must be so absorbed by position and occupation that he forgets that a sound life needs as much play as work. A person can, of course, add so much play into even a tedious profession that there is parity already in working life.

If this is not possible, one can locate the realm of play outside one's professional life. Nowadays there are numerous ways. Starting out from physical activities, there are the sports, and if one is prevented from participating, one can now more than ever participate vicariously by watching, for example, tennis or football on television.

One must always remember, however, that play should never get out of hand: excess of play can no longer be said to be a balancing partner of 'work'. If gambling becomes a single-minded and serious pursuit, the alarm bells should be ringing. It is then about time that one turns around and seeks out another form of pleasure. It is necessary to maintain a mixture of serious activity and joy and laughter. Just as one must take time to laugh one must take time to play. Body and soul need the relief to recuperate from the slings and arrows of daily chores often doing the same mundane job for hours at a stretch.

Create a 'double reality', live outer and dwell inner, thrive at a dual level, and develop a series of balances, which give purpose and meaning and makes life worth living.

63. The Mental Pendulum

The mind is located in the still middle of the psyche, but it cannot be expected that the psychic life should stay motionless there. There is traffic back and forth between the physical reality and the world of the soul. The movement of life can be likened to a pendulum swinging between opposite poles. It must be controlled that the oscillation does not turn extreme and gets out of control. Man can swing so far inwards that he reaches the boundary of the Divine, and so far outwards that he nears the region of the hells. When the zigzag is modest, he stays closer to his heart and remains more human.

Man must, as much as possible, be moderate and well-adjusted. He survives longer and is not envied. He should turn to Christ, Confucius and Buddha for gospels that preach measure and harmony in the world.

Movement cannot just be in one direction. Only swinging outward is as abnormal as only swinging inward. The saint in his cell is as much in error as the jet-set pleasure hunter. Either will end being aware of the melancholy of unbalanced life. In either case a vacuum is developing that is filled sooner or later with a feeling of halfness and loneliness.

On the shelf there are two figures, one representing the suffering Christ carrying his cross and the other the happy laughing Buddha holding a jug of wine, the first made of rough wood, the second of shining porcelain. They form a significant pair, the two extremes of life. Between them are as many rungs on the ladder as there are days in man's life from absolute happiness to utter suffering. There are the days of wine, song and poetry but also the days of hardship, pain and death. Man's life shifts, as he goes through the whole gamut from gaiety to grief and from grief to gaiety.

64. The Democratic Balance

The Balance must be sought and found within. A simile from the political, international world would be Switzerland. As early as 1515 Switzerland abandoned all territorial ambitions; she left the world to its own devices and decided that she should ever after arrive at equipoise within her own boundaries. She turned to her particular resources and has become an example for humanity. One can conclude that Switzerland was the first true democracy.[183] Nevertheless, she has not turned her back on the world. She has developed the political and social stability which has served the entire world and mankind. One paradox is that she has become a rich country, doubtlessly richer that she would have been if she had striven for political power outside her borders.

Today we find an increasing number of Swiss examples among the countries of the world. Any true democracy endeavours to live up to the basic ideas of tolerance and freedom and to attain its domestic equilibrium. Political parties and elections create a spectrum of power, and from election to election one can follow how the Balance moves within the spectrum. This has led to today's liberal, democratic order where the one-man-one-vote elections spell peace and order in more and more nations around the globe.

The world should work to follow the Swiss example and achieve the equilibrium that does not need an outer focus for stability.[184]

Good and evil join in man. He can do evil toward himself and toward others. The demon of evil is not least evident in the political world where it has been done in the name of God, the nation or the people; it can lead to Holocaust, Gulag and Srebrenica. Machiavelli (1469-1527) describes the "pest of power" in *Il Principe* (1521) and history teaches that it has always been the same when the power has been in the possession of a single ruler. Idealism has not proven enough to prevent evil to be done.[185]

---

[183] All the local and partial attempts at democracy first of all in the West but also in the East should not be forgotten. But as for true national democracy with wider franchise I dare say that Switzerland comes first and England next.

[184] Cf. R. Niebuhr (1892-1971): "Man's capacity for justice (= good) makes democracy possible; but man's inclination to injustice (= evil) makes democracy necessary." In R. Niebuhr 1944.

[185] "Evil" and "devil" are close in meaning and writing.

A society is necessary and needs to be adequately ruled by inspired men and women chosen in democratic elections. The one-vote-per-person power puts a check on political authority and channels it into local 'civil' war with party strife within borders. A new world is being created when power is counted with votes and not with guns. The nation achieves its balance by people's votes just like an individual achieves his balance by turning inwards.

65. Man's Two Souls

Goethe (1749-1832) writes in his *Faust*:

> Zwei Seelen wohnen, ach! in meiner Brust,
> Die eine will sich von den andern trennen:
> Die eine hält, in derber Liebeslust,
> Sich an die Welt mit klammernden Organen;
> Die andre hebt gewaltsam sich vom Dust
> Zu den Gefilden hoher Ahnen ...
>
> (Two souls, alas, cohabit in my breast
> A contract one of them desires to sever
> The one like a rough lover clings
> To the world with the tentacles of its senses;
> The other lifts itself to Elysian Fields
> Out of the mist on powerful wings ...)[186]

Through Goethe's Faust a modern man speaks. He visualises that there are two souls, the soul of the flesh and the soul of the spirit, that is, one material soul and one immaterial soul, in his breast and deplores the fact that there are two of them.[187] With these words Goethe summarises the West. In the East it is difficult to find a similar statement. Eastern people are *closer* to *another* statement in the Faust: "Grau, teurer Freund, ist alle Theorie, und grün des Lebens goldner Baum" ("Gray, my friend, is all theory, green is life's golden tree.").[188] Western tradition

---

[186] *Goethe's Faust*, in L. MacNeice 1972, p. 40.

[187] R. Browning also notes man's two souls, "God be thanked, the meanest of His creatures, Boast two soul-sides, one to face the world with, One to show a woman he loves her." Browning quoted in F. C. Happold 1963, p. 92.

[188] *Goethe's Werke*, vol. V, *Faust*, p. 66.

shows a widening division between the interior soul and exterior mind. One can talk about the beast mind which links with the world, and the soul mind that connects with the Eternal, and there is a rift between the two.

Man indeed possesses two forms of consciousness, which correspond to Goethe's two souls. There is the extrinsic consciousness, which corresponds to the outer "hardware" consciousness and Jung's Number One Personality. Then there is the intrinsic, inner "software" consciousness, which corresponds to Jung's Number Two Personality. It is this *latter* Personality that, ultimately, is man's first personality, the personality that is oceanic and gives purpose and value to his life. It follows its own divine intention. Jung's Number One Personality, outer consciousness, can only give temporary and transient meaning and certainty, and it does not encompass more than what a person's intellect deduces by inference. It seems that Jung puts the consciousnesses in the wrong order. The inner software consciousness should come first and the outer hardware consciousness second.

Goethe laments that this rift has cloven man in two and generated boredom and vacuity as the heart's essence has been neglected and even been declared to be non-existent.[189] What is needed today is that the two halves are brought together again. The rift must be bridged leaving no seams between soul, heart, mind and body. They constitute one entity, as they are complementary. In the East no such distinction between the within and the without is apparent. Faith and cognition cooperate, there being no division between the holy and the profane.

66. The Indian and Tibetan Examples

The great Operation of the Whole has been seen in yet other ways. In Indian thought the Balance emerged between Vishnu and Shiva as the two unifying forces of Creation. Vishnu is held to be the great provider of the universe. He is the centripetal tendency, the creator who holds all things together; Shiva, on the other hand, is the centrifugal tendency, also seen as the great destroyer. Together they represent the Will of the Whole and

[189] The inner essence has been declared "insubstantial" and death has become "standardised."

together they direct the natural course of the universe that is tuned to a cosmic harmony.

In Tibetan Tantra Buddhism the cosmic process is displayed in a simile using sensual symbols and metaphors. Creation is the great interaction of the male and the female. The active force is represented by the male phallus and the passive force is seen as the female vulva. The Eternal Will comes in the shape of a phallus and, in the vulva, all things are created naturally. A phallus in a vulva is then a symbol of the eternal in the temporal and the inner in the outer. The directing and creating Will cannot be exhibited in a better way than the phallus and the receiving outer cannot be represented with a better metaphor than the female vulva. This sort of speculation may seem reprehensible in cultures where erotic organs are only mentioned in hushed tones. However, careful deliberation leads one to the conclusion that this allegory expresses the cosmic harmony and order as good as any other. One can then also appreciate the pure delight the Tibetan Buddhist takes in scenes of the holy conjunction of copulation and in depictions of couples engaged in sexual intercourse. He envisages the wondrous Creation in such images.

67. Chance and Signals

Chance is to be lived. To follow the Signals and walk the Line, that is the aim. This may seem a tightrope performance, but it need not be. If Chance is allowed to serve, it will guide a person through each event and day. There must be no impediment in his heart, no dissociation between his interior unconscious heart and his exterior conscious mind. The linkage must be direct between the inspiration and the active day. If the door is left open to the deep regions of the psyche, Chance will tell him what course to take, and he need not err among the snares of circumstance.

Man is governed by the instinctive urges which are as real as the entelechy in any plant or animal. He is, however, more uprooted than plants and animals and in possession of his freedom of choice. "A plant must have roots below as sunlight above and roots must be grubby."[190]

[190] C. S. Lewis 1960, p. 14.

It is man's duty to be open and receptive to fresh insights and live as spontaneously as any other animate creature.

If the roots of a tree or a plant are cut, the tree or plant withers and dies and if an animal loses his instincts, he is an easy prey for the hunter. Likewise, if man loses his inborn guidance, he wilts and suffers. That every third European succumbs to depression and angst can only be due to this uprootedness and loss of bearings. That people grow, wither and die like any plant or animal is natural, but that they are at the mercy of entelechy like any plant or animal is more difficult to accept.

68. Aristotle's Entelechy

It was Aristotle (384-322 B.C.) who introduced 'entelechy' (*entelecheia*), 'interior law and purpose'. What this ancient Greek genius voiced was the idea that everything comes from within and has an intelligent purpose, beginning and end. "Everything is guided in a certain direction from within. ... The egg of the hen is internally designed and destined to become not a duck but a chick; the acorn becomes not a willow but an oak. The design is internal, and arises from the type and function of the thing."[191] Durant comments that *entelecheia* is "one of these magnificent Aristotelian terms which gather up into an entire philosophy."[192]

This inner Will is the Prime Mover, First Cause, the Master Designer or the Creator in accordance with culture, custom and language.[193] It is an organic process of birth, growth and decline that equals the ongoing evolution. It is Order, a Grand Balance, Randomness and Chance in and for itself!

Aristotle's universal perspective is not monopolised but belongs to every creed and religion. It requires only the private and personal effort of 'inscending' and 'being one with things,' leading to the "the love that is purest and sweetest, has a kiss of desire on the lips."[194]

---

[191] W. Durant 1953, p. 69.

[192] W. Durant, *ibid.*

[193] It is natural that man's imagination made human caricatures of the divine truth. As Xenophanes (570-480 B.C.) noticed: were donkeys devout they would imagine their gods as donkeys.

[194] John Boyle O'Reilly (1844-1890), in the poem *A White Rose.*

Aristotle visualises that the Absolute Will has an infinite direction and goal. Entelechy is not only the reason for all growth and life of plants and animals but also constitutes the godlike inspiration for all Creation. Thus, the wonder of consciousness extends not only to the great creative diversity at large but also to the minute details of daily living. If there are programmes for all the great forms, why should they not also exist for all the small forms? The great heavenly computer is big enough to comprise every thing, down to a cell and an atom. In human life this happens when the inner channel is open and the eternal programme is allowed to inspire behaviour. The Will acts seemingly without cause, and, therefore, in a worldly sense, it is accidental.[195] It is, however, neither accidental nor fortuitous but an acausal logic that manifests an entelechial Chance that deserves being written with a capital C.[196]

69. Emotions and Stress

Emotional stress endured over a long period of time is especially detrimental to health. As long as it is lived, it is perhaps not so severe, because it is ensconsed in the patterns of activities. Hatred, irritation, and active daily life shield man and woman from themselves, that is, from their subjective immediacy and inner wounds. Really, psychoses arise when the circumstances of stress are gone and they find themselves in new situations. Man's spiritual landscape can be as damaged by mental blows, as his body by physical fatigue. Then, he will discover that he has suffered psychic injury which remains with him, waking and sleeping, to the end of his days.

Anyone who leads an active life knows that all life is reflected and rerun in the dreams, the recondite language of the inner parts. The more intense the sensory occurrences are, the more strongly they recur in dreams. Emotions that are as large in magnitude as shock leave residues in a person's soul that only dissolve slowly and leave scars for the rest of his duration on earth.

---

[195] There is a divine logic above human logic that concerns also unconscious states, for example, dreams.

[196] Anton Zeilinger, in Dennis Overbye, *New Tests of Einstein's 'spooky' Reality*, in International Herald Tribune, 29 December, 2005, p. 9.

The conclusion is that one must not allow oneself to be exposed to events and sensations that are emotionally damaging and leave traces on the mind. This means that one ought to withdraw as soon as one becomes trapped in an emotional impasse. The withdrawal can be done in many ways. In this day and age there are indeed opportunities to back away from impossible situations and start afresh. This could prove to be difficult for many who are caught in position, power and wealth; and it can also be tempting to do battle and stand up for one's rights. However, one's health and cells are too precious for such ruthless treatment. When tried by circumstances and one's well-being is threatened, one had better leave things as they are, endeavour to forget – and move on.

Confucius put this neatly when he said: "When wanted, go; when not wanted, then hide."[197]

70. Run Man, Run!

On occasion when one meets someone who is trapped in an impossible situation, who is isolated, beset by enmity and persecuted by all and everybody, the urge rises to scream to him, "Run man, run!" At times one would like to play Coriolanus and quit when treated outrageously, bursting out: "There is a world elsewhere!"[198] People must recognise that "one can change one's location and leave a problem behind."[199] They owe it to life, they owe it to their inner selves.

It can be difficult to leave sad memories behind. Those ghosts in the memory storehouse, of course, endure, but they shrink and wither and need not influence a new place and a new milieu. Time and circumstances can heal damage as layer upon layer of new memories are piled on top of the sad remembrances and prevent them from rising to awareness. Even in dreams they gradually fade away.

A soul that is harmed can remain damaged. There can be a vicious circle of evil breeding evil, and damage nurturing damage. This cycle must be broken. Introspection, prayer, friends and even psychoanalysis

---

[197] *Lun Yü* VII: 10. My translation. Arthur Waley (1889-1966): "When wanted, then go; when set aside, then hide." (A. Waley 1938)

[198] *Coriolanus*, Act III. In W. Shakespeare 1937, p. 844.

[199] L. van der Post 1952, p. 162.

can be of good service. If one manages to cure one's soul, the rest will fall into place.

Wholesome social relations are vital. People must learn to be temperate and considerate within the circle they associate. One does not hurt others without hurting oneself. Nor does one nurture others without nurturing oneself.

71. The Unconscious, Instincts and Existential Roots

"What you get rid of last are the roots." This can indeed be said about the instincts that rule people more than we can imagine. The instincts feed them as much as food and sunshine. Similarly a tree is nourished as it stretches toward the sun but also receives nourishment from the earth.[200] When one sees a tulip growing again from the same bulb, can one have any doubt about there being a programme deep inside? The Purpose is there, directing the entire process of growth and transformation. The Heavenly Will that Chinese speak about is the organic energy reaching out to every atomic particle.

Humans are ripped loose from the ground as they move freely on legs, but this does not mean that they do not have a matrix from where all growth is programmed and directed. They have their roots of existence, which are as important and real for them as roots are for the trees. "Cutting himself off from his inner nature, man cuts himself off from the roots of his Being."[201]

It might accordingly be seen as a strange sort of mental aberration when man today neglects and even fights his intuitive mind. It is a form of affliction that is becoming global as the scientific mentality overruns the world. The subjective consciousness is often declared non-existent, but it cannot be. It will always be there, and the more it is neglected the more it will scream. The Age of Reason is a good example. The more reason was worshipped the more irrationally people behaved. One can study the life of any great Philosopher, and one will discover that new

[200] Henry David Thoreau expressed: "probe the earth to see where your main roots run." See R. Dickens 1974, p. 11.

[201] W. Barrett 1962, p. 126

kinds of unreason crept in through the back door.[202] The French Revolution wilth its guillotine, the final fruit of the French Raison, is indicative of a new ungodly reason.

72. The Divine Will

The Divine Will manifests itself in many ways. It flows forth and it directs. It emanates from the divine quality of being and creates the fullness of life. It offers guidelines to what is right and following its advice one need not suffer desolation, alienation and disillusionment of the exterior world. It is when the direction is guided by worldly values, lust, egotism and greed, that the equilibrium is lost.

When the Will is allowed to direct our actions, it cuts through the dilemmas of everyday problems. It steers, and however rough and demanding the going is, one can see, once the day comes to a close, that the Will willed rightly. It is as if the day composed itself. On the other hand, when external factors are allowed to decide, the actions and decisions often take a wrongful course. They do not then have the quality of being guided by inner inspiration. This does not mean that other-directed decisions need be wrong. As long as they reflect sympathy and empathy, they bear the hallmark of the all-embracing Will. It is as if the Will works spontaneously through both natural and rational avenues.[203]

We create aloneness, alienation and estrangement from ourselves and from the world in which we live, when we deprive the Will of its primary function. The authentic life vanishes and relative and transitory values become dominant, when the focus is one-sidedly on the conditional world.[204]

---

[202] "Refused admission at the front door, the spirits come in by force or stealth from the rear." L. van der Post 1978, p. 19. Cf. *Luke*, 11: 24-26.

[203] "Neglecting the internal and devoting oneself to the external, one loses one's purpose in life, one becomes broad but lacks essentials." L. van der Post 1978, p. 185. That rational social action may lead to Balance is well described by I. Hedenius 1964, pp. 121-122f.

[204] Nationalism, political fanaticism, idealism, sports, and numerous other activities can serve as ersatz activities. Like fame and name they may spell meaning in man's life on earth. They might give satisfaction temporarily but not in the long run. You may climb Mount Everest but up there you might feel that the

73. Jung's Magnolia Tree

The most beautiful allegory of what life should be like derives from Jung, and is related by his friend Laurens van der Post.[205] In a dream Jung sees a city square with a round pool. In its midst there is a small island, drenched in sunlight, and "in the middle of the island stands a splendid magnolia exploding into flower with reddish flames which add a light of their own to that of the sun."[206]

In this dream Jung sees the great truth that has been expressed here. The city square stands for the outer and the round pool for the inner truth. The island represents the existential core of man, and the magnolia the Eternal Will that shoots from its midst. The magnolia with its resplendent flowers is the most beautiful symbol for the spirit, when it is allowed to flow through man's psyche and flower in life. Van der Post says, "We have all an island self with a tree of life in flower."[207]

We have the tree, but it is up to the individual to ensure that it is allowed to bloom. More often than not, we seem to stunt the buds so that it does not bloom. Alternatively, we bury the entire island under rubbish from the city square so that the island cannot act as the central part of ourselves. This is perhaps the great tragedy of modern culture which lets gasoline vapours poison the total city square, swamping the island with debris and preventing the gorgeous magnolia to come into bloom and display its magnificent flowers.

74. The Magnolia and the Spirit of the East

Jung sees the magnolia as a symbol of the spirit of the East. He visualises how Indian, Chinese and Japanese wisdom will infiltrate the spiritually impoverished West. The East stands for the spiritual whole and the West for the material parts.

---

mountain looks better from below. At the end of the day, all these activities might just signify spiritual dearth!

[205] Cf. L. van der Post 1978, p. 185f.

[206] *Ibid.*

[207] *Ibid.*

The West is ahead in the outer sector but has fallen behind in the inner sector. It is then natural that the East learns from the West and the West from the East. The East can learn about the Part, and the West can learn about the Whole.

The magnolia flowers "exploded with reddish flames which added a light of their own to that of the sun." This is a lovely picture of the person who is attuned to the divine light of his heart. He explodes "with reddish flames which add to the light of the sun." Jung had come to the realization, that intuition was a driving, blazing light in man's life. He had felt the spirit and strength of the subliminal that comes in one explosion after another like the the magnolia flowers which burst open in the spring!

Personal experience must come first. Allegories and parables come afterwards. If Jung's dream were merely recognised as a philosophical account, which is common the present day, it would, ultimately, be devoid of meaning. It would be a mere chronicle without deeper significance. His dream would function little more than a *mandala* or a cross in a museum. What is needed urgently is that individuals, inspired by the truth of Jung's dream, establish contact with the Eternal during their precious duration on earth. Without that effort, it does not help however well they apprehend the verity of a blazing magnolia.

75. The One-dimensional Man

Modern man has become the naked ape, one-dimensional with only reason and intellect at his disposal. The old faith is gone, and the new belief in constant progress is a chimera. Its Napoleonic overtones seems to end him up on St. Helena. He needs desperately to "regain a purpose, which bears on eternity" and "opens up a meaningful world," and be the two-dimensional individual he was through the ages.[208]

This was not a problem until the Renaissance. Throughout the Middle Ages the interior psychic phenomena were yet a living reality. They were not shadows but the dominant partners in human undertakings. In Jungian terms, there was during these ages there was the worship of

[208] Jung seems optimistic of things to come. He says that the material optimism, the self-consciousness and arrogance of the 20th century are diminishing and that our world is ready for a new world – also spiritually.

woman (Mary) side by side with the worship of man (Christ). A new tradition in philosophy began with Descartes and his dream in 1619. He was the first thinker to assert a sharp separation of mind and matter, asking for scientific clarity and certainty. The present malady of man is the result of the following four centuries. Man's interior world has shrunk while his exterior world has expanded. Reason has taken over and the world has become cold and rational.

It is of interest that China since early times went through a similar developmental process. With the preponderance of Confucian thought from the first Han dynasty (220-206 B.C.), the Chinese society became rational and masculine, and female values were curtailed. Other creeds, however, sustained the sanity of the Chinese soul. China never became religiously monolithic like Europe. Side by side with male Confucianism there was always female Taoism and close to Taoism was Buddhism with its sublime Middle Path teachings. The Chinese could always lead double lives, denied the Westerner, in which aesthetics and morality merged. He never needed to suffer from a bad conscience like the western man. He tended to Confucianism in daily life, to Buddhism in life's *Grenzsituationen* and to Taoism in art and poetic life. The same happened in Japan where a masculine *samurai* world came to dominate from the twelfth century. *Zen* aesthetics, Buddhism and earlier Shinto values provided, however, a feminine dimension and symmetry to society and individual life.[209]

---

[209] The West tended to absolute moral commandments from equally absolute prophets, Moses in Judaism, Christ in Christianity and Muhammed in Islam, and the East inclined to liberal moral rules. Hinduism, Buddhism, Taoism and Confucianism have doctrines but no absolute teachers. The result is that the East shows less religious egotism than the West where prophets demand total loyalty. It is surprising, then, that liberal thinking developed in the West and not in the East. Scientific materialism, market economy and political democracy grew in the West on the foundation of the Christian gospel on the worth of the individual – in spite of priests and churches. Thereupon, human greed and competition have done the job, the result of which can be witnessed in international science, economic globalisation and democratic rule in 121 of the world's 192 nations (as of 2008).

76. Two Halves or One Whole

What is torn can be repaired. The two ends of a broken bone can grow together again. The disrupted psyche can, likewise, reunite and form a new harmonious whole. What is sundered becomes unified and the soul becomes sound again. The mind must turn inward until it reaches the existential point between reason and feeling, where the infinite and the finite meet and merge. One-sidedness vanishes, and however the pendulum swings from one pole to the other, it remains a sound dialectic movement. One is guided in this mental calmness, and the intellect is directed through the tangle of daily endeavours. 'Frustration', 'depression', 'neurosis' and 'boredom' are eliminated. When one begins to feel things negatively, one knows that it is time for the vision to be renewed – and for the grand feeling to flood the mind again.

Oneness and harmony must be the aim of man's striving. He must realise a self that is greater than his interior and exterior together. The sum of the whole always adds up to more than the sum of its parts.[210] He must cut through the tops and valleys of his mental process and realise that higher harmony and unity which encloses all outer and all inner. Then he will be aware of his capacities and characteristics, which constitute his essence. His ego will not block what is on the inside, and will not make the supernatural world appear only in the form of a dark and threatening shadow – a shadow which cannot be shaken off any more than earthly shadows.

This vision of the Whole has been experienced in religion through the millennia the world over. Man has been tied to it through myth, magic and ceremonies. Today, only the shadow of the inner side remains in the western mind. Schools have turned secular and religious education is gone. No hymns are heard, no prayers are read and no ethics is taught whereas worldly and secular subjects are given most of the time and attention. From a reality where "God was the measure of all things" man has moved to a world where "he is the measure of all things." As a result, the temples loom forlorn and empty while the queues at the psychiatrists have grown long.

---

[210] Just as a tune is something more than the mere sum of its parts. H. Hawton 1956, p. 142.

D. Lack says, "Either man, like other animals, has no part to his nature, or, as in the Christian view, a supernatural event took place at the time of man's first appearance, before which our ancestors were proto-human mammals, and after which, through the gift of the soul, they were truly human."[211]

J. C. Eccles (1903-1997) says, "Each Soul is a new Divine Creation which is implanted into the growing foetus at some time between conception and birth. It is the certainty of the core of unique individuality that necessitates the 'Divine Creation'. I submit that no other explanation is tenable; neither the genetic uniqueness with its fantastically impossible lottery, nor the environmental differentiations which do not determine one's uniqueness, but merely modify it."[212]

So speak Christian Darwinists. Darwin is limited to the outer and the eternal to the inner.[213] Chance is in the driver's seat. It is, however, not a blind randomness but a higher logic that follows laws which we are not able to decipher. One is reminded of Xenophanes' words:

> The gods did not reveal, from the beginning,
> All things to us; but in course of time,
> Through seeking, men find that which is better.
> But as for certain truth, no man has known it,
> Nor will he know it ...

Absolute certainty will never be the lot of man. Chance sees to that.[214] But Balance first and Chance afterwards can make a happy life.

77. The Eternal and God

The Eternal is regarded in as many ways as there are religions on earth and given as many names. One thing the names have in common. They all refer to the Whole, seen in pantheistic, polytheistic, monotheistic, animistic or other ways.

---

[211] D. Lack 1961, pp. 88-89, quoted in J. C. Eccles 1989, p. 235.

[212] J. C. Eccles 1989, p. 240.

[213] Darwin took no interest in metaphysics, but advancing and professing natural selection, he seems to have believed in an intelligence (and perhaps a purpose) behind things.

[214] R. H. Torrance 1994, p. 276.

The Eternal in religion and expressed in philosophers' thought can be of equal interest. Neither should be dismissed. People's beliefs expound the absolute truth in subjective terms while philosophers offer the same in objective terms. Apart or together they teach what makes life worth living. As Indian wisdom teaches: "Like a bee gathering honey from different flowers, we should seek the good in different scriptures and all religions."[215]

One can draw a line round the globe and place what belongs to the Eternal above the line and what belongs to Earth below the line. Someone might ask about the whereabouts of the line. Where time and space begin is below the line and where time and space end is above the line. The Chinese have two terms for the same: *hsing-chih-shang*, Jap. *keijijô*, 'what is above (without) shapes' (metaphysical), and *hsing-chih-hsia*, Jap. *keijika*, 'what is below (with) shapes' (physical). Form and shape make the difference between what is eternal and what is temporal. They also divided reality in essence (*ch'i*, Jap. *ki*) and principle (*li*, Jap. *ri*). This thinking was the world-view of the Confucian mandarins up to our own time.

Analogously, it is easy to follow the thought in the West from earliest age and find the search for the Eternal both in common religion and in sublime philosophy. In Greece it can be pursued from Parmenides and Heraclitus until Plato (ca. 428-348 B.C.), Aristotle and Plotinus. Most of western philosophy can afterwards indeed be described as a series of footnotes to Plato. The psycho-physical dualism of the Eternal and the Temporal is given in much variety, the medieval God and his Creation, Descartes' mental and physical realms (1641), Spinoza's substance and modes (1675), Leibniz's monads and vitalism (1714),[216] Kant's noumena and phenomena (1781) and so forth.

The great transformation came with the Enlightenment and Naturalism when European culture was set adrift from its medieval roots and the Eternal was reduced and even denied. This led to a focus on the external world at the expense of self-knowledge. Philosophers have been anatomizing the Temporal while the Eternal has been forgotten. For

---

[215] Quotation in J. C. Cooper 1981, p. 84. The Indian source is given as *Srimad Bhagavatam*.

[216] The monads are the "true atoms of nature" (Leibniz), similar to the *ki* in Chinese Neo-Confucian thinking (Chu Hsi).

most people around the globe, however, the Eternal is still real both in life and in death.[217]

78. The Will in Things

When one experiences the Will that flows through the All, one apprehends that there is no separation of the noumenal and phenomenal worlds. One senses an infinite direction and a suprarational activity and one is aware of belonging to an endless process of Creation. One sees the sacred everywhere, in a 'grain of sand' (William Blake) and in a 'flower on the crannied wall' (Alfred Tennyson, 1809-1892). One understands the Indian who cannot conceive of Nietzsche's "God is dead" and refuses to discuss the subject with sceptical westerners. He finds no reason to ponder whether it is a matter of empiricism or psychism – being or nothing.

The Will embraces all things and mirrors the All. Looking up into the crown of a tree, one has the loveliest picture of the Will. Every branch and twig speaks about the wonder of Creation, and each pattern surpasses all human art. Likewise, the Will begets in each of us distinct forms that are unmatchable. Hence, any streamlining and alignment is as futile as attempts to shape the growth of the trees. No matter what efforts are made, the distinctive traits of each tree will remain.[218] Likewise, no two days are identical, no two nights, no two halves of a face. Nothing really is repeated in exact detail. The Will is at the root of this miracle. There is spontaneity and individuality in all Creation. Everything is in harmony with destined order. It is entelechial, also in man – whose 'free will' is, in the main, a delusion.

Man is more prone to see the square than the circle. Both East and West man has striven to seek order and meaning in things and the unity of nature; he has picked up what has been square and digital and left out what is circular and analogue. In society he has behaved in a similar fashion, and instead of letting things run their natural course, he has

---

[217] D. Loy 2000, p. 40.

[218] As a child this writer was astonished that he could not find two blades of grass that were identical. He was as astonished as a grown-up to learn that two finger prints are never alike.

forced them into cruel strait jackets and produced conformity. Plainer the Chinese way which sees the square and the circle as complementary![219]

79. The Garden of Eden and the Age of Cronos

Man has always longed for constancy and stability and philosophers East and West have dreamed of Utopias and unchanging Edens. They have observed unspoilt forms in nature and expected the same in their societies. The Chinese tried to force natural phenomena into coherent, often numerical, systems. Human society was treated in the same manner: there had been an age of Sages at the beginning of history, and it was the responsibility of each scholar and statesman, not to mention the Emperor, to practice benevolent government and sustain the eternal order that admits of no change. Change spelled abnormalities and calamities such as floods, drought, famine and disease.

The West presents an interesting parallel. In ancient Palestine and Greece one finds an original perfect era when everything was constant and static. In Hebrew tradition it was the Garden of Eden and in Greece the Age of Cronos, when society was blissfully Divine and change did not occur. Plato harks back to this age as he visualises Eternal Ideas, among them the 'Idea of the State', all emanating from the Eternal and unfolding as secondary Forms.

We can visit people on any continent and discover that constancy, in one shape or another, is fundamental to all of them. A wider perspective would reveal that we do not recognise constancies around us but an infinity of occurrences and processes, coming and going cyclically.

Change is thus a recent phenomenon in the world. Until the Renaissance it was the static world-view that man sought in the Bible and the ancient classics. The Renaissance itself was an attempt to revive ancient perfect forms of culture. It ended, however, by creating a new world-view of change that has propelled the West first and now the whole world to constant progress in a crescendo of new science and material learning that is not necessarily for the better.

---

[219] Mencius says, "He who knows his nature knows Heaven; to nourish one's nature is Heaven."

80. The Scientists and the Creation

When exploring reality one might be inclined to think that "it is written in mathematical language" (Galileo Galilei, 1564-1642). Science has come a long way since Galileo penned these words, and an immense volume of structured order has been brought forth. We can anticipate a further crescendo of new discoveries in decades to come. Unfortunately, however, often in a language that is impossible for most of us to understand. Take for example the formulas of relativity by Albert Einstein? How many people genuinely understand them?

Even though not always a blessing, the rise of science is undoubtedly a gift to mankind. It is the finest achievement of human culture, the effect of rigid observations and experimentally verified theories. Its discoveries constitute the most significant accomplishment of man. It has cleansed his thinking of unnatural beliefs and occult sciences have faded away. Earthquakes and meteors are no longer ascribed to mystical intervention, witches are no longer burned at the stake and epidemic diseases are not attributed to man's sin. "There is even something commendable about a psychological method – psychoanalysis – which cures mental afflictions by making the unconscious conscious."[220]

It is the Eternal Will, also in scientific learning, that makes people realise that all reality is tightly bound together by well defined laws. If the dicta of science manifest the regularities within the processes and make man feel the eternal propinquity of all things, his soul makes him aware of the irrational other side of what is instantly rational. Man is equipped to feel and apprehend the Will operating through Chance. It might not agree with common logic but there is yet a logic! Scientists have tried to express the immensity of the experience. Einstein, for example, could not help being astounded when confronting the incredible cosmic harmony. He writes that "it is a religious feeling that reveals such a superior reason and infinite intelligence that all human propensities are nothing but trivial and insignificant reflections of them."[221]

---

[220] M. Ricard 2006, p. 113.
[221] A. Einstein 1934, p. 21.

81. Similarities, East and West

That religious speculation is similar in such distant places and cultures as in India, China and Europe is astonishing. That East and West should have influenced each other is out of the question. In early times when basic thinking was born, communications were rare and, if any, served the world of commerce and seldom the world of ideas. The similarities must arise from the fact that approximately the same questions were raised on either side of the Eurasian continent.

This treatise forwards the following triad: the Eternal and its Will, Balance and Chance. These three concepts palpably reflect both western and eastern thought. The Judaeo-Christian-Islamic religions, originating from Abraham, with an anthropomorphic God, are not much different. If one exchanges God for the Eternal, the scriptures for the Will and the law for Balance, the teaching is much the same. The Christian religion has the categories of God, Christ and the Word, the Islamic religion has God, Muhammed and the Koran and the Greek philosopher Plotinus (ca. 204-270) propounds the existence of a group of Three (Hypostases): the One, the Soul and the Intellect.

Heaven and the Way[222]existed above things in China in the same manner as the Gods and Destiny in Greece. In Chinese thought, last advanced by Chu Hsi (1130-1200), one meets the threefold metaphysics: Heaven (*t'ien*, *ten*) and its Way (*tao*) above, energy-matter (*ch'i*, *ki*) below and the heart-mind (*shin*, *kokoro*). Heaven's *Tao* combined Balance and Chance, equalling the *li* and *ch'i* of Chu Hsi thought.[223] Chu Hsi envisaged the implicit unity in explicit duality, in which *ch'i*, energy-matter, concurred with *li*, 'orderly principle.' In India the emphasis was on the oneness of things and the phenomenal world which was regarded as illusory. Metaphysics presided over physics.[224]

---

[222] Heaven has been defined as "a cosmic moral order and a being or power, possessing intelligence and will, which guides impartially the destinies of men." *Sources of Chinese Tradition*, vol. 1, p. 6. The Way (*tao*) is the cosmic order in Taoist thought.

[223] See L. Kohn 1992, pp. 45-50. In other contexts, *Tao* equals "thusness" in Buddhist thought and *jen*, "compassion" or "goodness" in Confucian thought. See also F. S. C. Northrop 1946, p. 350.

[224] The oneness of things is in the centre of religions generally. Scriptures and sages of all ages speak with one voice about the "all in all" and the "one being the all

Modern Western thought resides mainly within physics while metaphysics is negated. If metaphysics is discussed, this is done with much caution, scepticism and often even disdain.[225] The war waged upon superstition and backwardness has resulted in a demand for scientific proof as regards also religion. In the East people combined the affective (heart), the cognitive (mind) and the intuitive (soul). No conflict between science and religion was ever apparent. The inner psychic landscape was as important as the outer affective and cognitive world. Metaphysics was considered the highest form of knowledge. From intuition to cognition came the comprehension that the individual was united with other beings, animals and plants, all forming a 'single, harmonious and cooperating whole.'[226]

82. Faith or Knowledge

The discussion in this œuvre has been structured to avoid overflowing into a discourse on faith and a personal God. The discussion has focused on divine knowledge while the existence or non-existence of a God has not been under debate. Interest in this question diminishes, as soon as one experiences the light within and goes from faith to knowledge.

When one dwells on the line where the inner and outer meet, all talk about faith loses importance. Balance is not faith because faith is not involved, neither is it reason because reason is equally not involved. It is knowledge that subsumes both faith and reason. All talk about transcendent order, a personal God, and someone 'up there' becomes superfluous.

In Balance one realises that one is part of a supernatural logic that is continuous within and without, whether called one thing or another. One can quote from Jung and agree: "I cannot define what God is. I can

---

in all." Today modern physics joins them by describing how elementary particles and energy unite in a pervasive weave. See, for example, M. Planck 1944, pp. 298-299.

225 Metaphysical is today mostly equated with "untestable" and "unscientific."

226 W. H. Walsh 1963, pp. 1-19 and D. Loy 2000, pp. 154-172. Last quotation from H. G. Creel 1929, p. 47, that continues, "every part of which properly and ideally worked toward a common end and the welfare of all."

only tell you that my work has established that this pattern has at its disposal the greatest transformative energies of life."[227] Once reality is comprehended in this light, one tends to agree with Jung, saying, "Ich glaube nicht, ich weiss" ("I do not believe, I know").[228] Jung stands in contrast to Sigmund Freud who described God as 'nothing but an insubstantial shadow.'[229]

What is needed is the cultivation of the interior. If one lives and breathes inner harmony, seeing oneself in the centre of the Whole, one need not worry about the Eternal being named one way or another. The inner knowledge unifies the knower and the known. When one senses that all existence is holy what need is there to debate whether it is one thing or another? Intellectuals can speculate whether it is naturalism or idealism! At the end of the day, it is a single person who listens to the voice within intuiting and instructing! If the harmony is disturbed and one lives without the inner light, one's life is affected and one's happiness vanishes.

83. Panholiism

All reality is holy and as Jung says, "God is so great that it is utterly impossible to add to or subtract from his greatness." This is expressed already in the opening book of the Old Testament, *Genesis*, where the voice (Yahweh) in the bush informs Moses, "I am who or what I am." This statement can easily be interpreted as "One who is" or "That which is." Reality is a 'panholiism' (or '*hylozôism*', '*panpsychism*' or '*pan(en)-theism*'[230]) that embraces all reality, what is visible and what is invisible, chaos and cosmos. The 'panholiism' is experienced as Purpose, Order and Balance and revealed in the great laws of the universe. There is

---

[227] In a letter to L. van der Post. See L. van der Post 1982, p. 351.

[228] C. G. Jung, quoted in L. van der Post 1978, p. 85. "That is the truth of it – that we all know, God, that we know, that we know, we know, we know." S. Bellow 1970, p. 252.

[229] D. C. Dennet 2006, p. 7.

[230] Panentheism is a term used by E. Troeltsch in S. Coakley 1988, p. 116. *Panpsychism* expresses that all matter has soul in, for example, pre-Socratic philosophy, in Spinoza's *Ethics*, in Leibniz's monologue and in Chinese *ki* thinking. See K. R. Popper and J. C. Eccles 1977, p. 53, and O. G. Lidin 2006, pp. 19-32.

cause and effect, there is gravity, there is electromagnetism, relativity, the quantum theory, and other laws discovered and often honoured by Nobel prizes. Leading biologists and physicists tend to vitalist pantheism. Their science ends up "in pure mentalism which is independent of the existence of any external world whatever."[231] They aim at absolute truth as much as does true religion. "Besides the laws of physics some other principle must be at work in the living organism."[232]

In western religions a Creator is recognised above all existence.[233] One meets a personal God in the Hebrew, Christian and Muslim creeds. Whether referred to as God, Yahweh or Allah He is an anthropomorphic being. In eastern beliefs the Eternal has been taken impersonally, as what one breathes in and what one breathes out, a *Tao* above things, as *li* and *ch'i* in things or an all-pervading animism. It has not been a personal God referred to with the pronoun He but rather a Something, referred to as the absolute truth.

St. Anselm (1033-1109) articulated the plenitude of the Eternal with his words *maius cogitari non potest* ('that Being greater than which none can be conceived'). St. Anselm realised that "no amount of knowing diminishes the amount of the unknown." St. Anselm was referring to the Christian God, but his words could equally be a description of the 'panholiism'.

Then what about prayer? Prayer serves a precious function, when it is directed to the Eternal or God under any name, in contemplative silence or in spoken words. It remains close to reflection and introspection as a means to maintain the harmony of life – not least in times of crisis. "It helps also when one does not believe in it", as N. Bohr says about the horseshoe hung above the door in his summer house.

84. The Eternal is Love and Compassion

'Love' is one of the most used and abused terms in any language, utilised in multifarious senses. It finds mention as much in profane as in religious contexts. From Hildegard of Bingen to the Beatles hardly a song,

---

[231] W. R. Inge 1925, p. 365.
[232] G. E. Stahl (1660-1734), quoted in M. Nagy 1991, p. 237.
[233] See, for example, K. Armstrong 1993, p. 309.

drama or novel has been written without exploiting it. It is used no less to effect in sacred contexts. As a notion in Christian vocabulary it features in all the gospels, and hardly a sermon is preached that does not mention it. In essence absolute love equates God and is synonymous with the Eternal. It is central among virtues and on an equal footing with Heaven in Confucian thought. In Plato's thought pure love joins everlasting beauty and in Plotinus' thought it is equal to the One. Love is so central in the life of Balance that it need not be mentioned often and passionately. If a person is guided by interior Peace, and the Will stretches into outward life, selfless love and goodness will result. Oscar Wilde wrote, "The consciousness of loving and being loved brings warmth and richness to life that nothing else can bring."

Love flows from within and is expressed in compassion, the common denominator of all creeds. When the Eternal Will moves and acts, our lives merge and goodness triumphs. It forms one straight line from the inside to the outside.[234] At times the final result might seem harsh. This is possible because the Will may seem inscrutable and its directives may surprise and afflict. Occasionally, it seems even to contradict love and compassion. However, the Will never gives orders beyond what is said in the Bible that "God is love and he that dwelleth in love dwelleth in God and God in him."[235]

Today sex and love are intermingled in entertainment and love seems to come second to sex. It is forgotten that the sex drive is rooted in the brain while true love is an outpour of the heart and soul. In the olden days a drama rarely deviated from love and compassion while intimate matters even nearing sex were unmentioned or only hinted at. Not so today when the bar is lowered.[236]

---

[234] W. Blake has described the inner-outer line of love and compassion in the poem with the title, "The Divine Image." Its central verse reads:

For Mercy, Pity, Peace, and Love
Is God, our father dear;
And Mercy, Pity, Peace, and Love
Is Man, his child and care.

In J. Hayward 1956, p. 240.

[235] 1 *John*, 4: 16.

[236] Today sex is the "opiate for the masses", not religion. Sex in man has come to equal sex among animals. The overemphasis of sexuality is an indication of the lack of values of our time.

85. Heart and Rotten Reins

When someone relies only on his heart for the truth, how can he be certain that it is not just self-deception? Did not a Chinese philosopher once say that relying on one's heart is like relying on 'rotten reins' when riding a horse? This was the Chinese philosopher's Hsün Tzu's (ca. 371-289 B.C.) opinion. It should not be forgotten, however, that most Chinese philosophers believed in the ceaseless outpouring of celestial goodness. Now, the proof is that Chance operates in a person's daily life in great or small things. Whether it comes to the longer perspective of an entire life or to the shorter perspective of a day, a mosaic of things and events unfold as the result of Chance, and when all the pieces fit together, they form a symmetry. Once one feels the harmony of the mosaic, one knows that one is on the right track. When even difficult problems are solved naturally, things fall into place, and the cogs mesh, one knows that divine fortuity operates in one's life.

If on the other hand the mosaic is in disorder, a whole array of signs are alerting a person that there is a kink on the line. When intuition is hindered by a dislodged harmony, it is time for retreat, for contemplation, for rest and sleep to reconquer the harmony within. Life will serve reminders whether one is in or out of balance and lives with or against nature.

Hsün Tzu says in one of his best passages that when the heart, that is, the inner is in disorder, "the mouth may hold good food, but it will not taste it; the ears may hear bells and drums, but they will not hear the music; the eyes may behold fine embroidery, but they will not see its pattern; one may wear the most comfortable clothing and sit on an even mat, but his body will be oblivious of them. Even if all the pleasant things in the world were offered to one in this state, he could not be content. ... Such is the lot of those who seek material things. ..."

On the other hand, Hsün Tzu continues, "When a man's heart is peaceful and happy, then even sights below the ordinary will satisfy the eye; even sounds below the ordinary will content the ear; coarse rice, vegetables and soup will be enough for the mouth; clothing of coarse cloth and sandals made from rough cords will give comfort to the body; a hut of straw, with a mat on the floor and a smattered stool to lean against, will suffice. Such a man, lacking all the fine things in the world, is yet happy. ... If he were appointed to rule the empire, it would mean much for the empire, but it would mean little difference in his peace of mind. This may indeed be called giving due weight to one's self, and making material things one's servants."[237]

86. Chance "bloweth where it listeth"

At the end of the day, a life led in harmony with Chance and Balance defies description. It has a numinous connection that cannot be apprehended with words nor grasped with intellectual activity. A passage from the gospel according to John neatly expresses this situation (*John*, 3: 8):

> The wind bloweth where it listeth,
> And Thou hearest the sound thereof,
> But canst not tell whence it cometh,
> And whither it goeth: so is everyone
> That is born by the Spirit.

This is as close as one can come to a description of the inborn life that moves unmapped by mundane and profane affairs and influences. One cannot force it, only open the heart and mind to it. Christ never put it better, and his words are only matched by the greatest eastern thinkers, as in the case of Lao Tzu who speaks of 'actionless activity', of 'everything becoming such as it is of itself' and of 'the spirit for ever functioning without any effort.'[238] We should not forsake the bliss of knowing that "where the Spirit of the Lord is, there is freedom" (2 *Corinthians*, 3: 17). Truly, intuited freedom is 'freedom's self' (Mary W. Shelley, 1797-1851). When heart and mind cooperate and respond spontaneously like leaves in the wind, few laws are required. In fact, most regulations could be scrapped, and few police would be required on the streets. When there are many regulations it is also better to rely on inspiration – and common sense – than to try to know them all.

---

[237] Translation by J. J. L. Duyvendak 1924, pp. 252-253, quoted in H. G. Creel 1953, pp. 109-110. Translation adapted.

[238] *Lao Tzu*, ch. 2-3.

87. Life and the Persian Rug

True life can be likened to a Persian rug with a pattern like no other. The pattern of existence should spread naturally throughout a life-span, just as the universe spreads artlessly over time. This should not be taken for granted. It is a mystery how things, both organic and inorganic, find their places in the biological order that extends to every global cell and atom. Chance is the warp and Balance the weft in all evolution.

Chance operates in the same inscrutable way in the warp and weft of a private life. One should strive to lead the life in line with the inner voice as it conducts the music of each single day. If one plays by ear, lucky happenstance will operate in one's life. The mystery of 'luck' is a characteristic of Chance under circumstances that cannot be explained. At such times it seems as though things happen at random at the appropriate time. It is said that when you are focused on something, avenues open up and intuition works on piled up facts. This is generally true. Intuitions are usually the long-awaited fruits of long and hard work. How many Nobel-prizes testify to that!

Guidance seems to spring from the depths of the human inner.[239] The right person can be in front of you at the time that he is mostly needed, the right book is suddenly just there, or the right opportunity presents itself at the crucial time. Just a little earlier or a little later would have been too early or too late; it happens at the very instant of need and cannot be explained by reason. It is Providence working, it is the Will directing me! In the quiet solitude the inner voice instructs in many ways at unforeseen times. "Wrap your spirit (*shen*) in stillness; then your body will become correct. You must remain calm and empty. Do not overwork your body; do not allow your vitality to become drained. Then you will live long."[240]

[239] Henri Bergson, among others, has stressed the importance of intuition in life. See, for example, H. Bergson 1929a.

[240] *Chuang Tzu*, ch. 11; quotation in Da Liu 1979, p. 97. Adapted.

88. Coincidence and Synchronicity

Walking the road of Balance, Chance presents man with uncommon encounters, which he can seize and accept – or ignore and reject. They happen instantaneously and fit in with life mysteriously and inexplainably. Man is free to comply with them, and will find that there is meaning in even the most trivial events. Alternatively, he can decide against pursuing the transcendent signals 'with the feel of wings'[241], and only follow his objective and well-informed cognition. The latter alternative seems in our present world to be predominant.

Such coincidences[242] most people experience without being aware of them. "They tend to pass over them as amazing but accidental" events.[243] For the believer they are proof that one is on the same wavelength with the true life; for the non-believer they are just 'chance'. One way or another they colour life. People do often not perceive them in the sacred light they deserve. Happy singular moments should be remembered and savoured. They merit consideration as unexpected blessings from the world beyond. Rather than forgetting them, one should go so far as writing them down. They are blissful happenings, giving pleasure to often humdrum life, the memory of them adds sparkle to one's spirit. "We ignore them at our peril,"[244] these resplendent occurrences of our lives and suffer for it!

A moment's consideration of the twentieth century will confirm that in no earlier age has well-informed cognition caused worse carnage and, truly, no earlier age has seen more need for humans who act on the inspired promptings of their inner.

89. Chance or a Machine

Living up to the signals from one's inner self lends richness and fullness. Imagine how dreary, how dull life is when all is planned by worldly

---

[241] *In Mountain Air*, poem by Glenn Ward Dresbach (1889-1968).
[242] Synchronism is another term for coincidence, used by Jung.
[243] M. Nagy 1991, p. 184. She says further, with reference to Jung, "They reveal an underlying a priori acausal orderedness."
[244] L. van der Post 1978, p. 50.

standards! This is exactly what is happening today. The entire life is rationalised in a geometrical fashion exponentially with sets of rules which are becoming more and more elaborate. The social sciences expand, as bureaucrats weave plans for everyone.

The total design of a person's brief span of life from cradle to grave is routinised. Rather than being an individual he becomes a computerised, numerical statistic. He is put on the Procrustean bed on which all humans are cut alike. A person is slowly dehumanised in a digital setting with norms and standards for life and thought. Not only has the world become a machine, but man has become a machine, too. And worse, he seems satisfied to be a machine, living in a machine and acting like a machine! He becomes one-dimensional as his "integral being is lost."[245] His existence becomes essentially empty and desolate and he forgets that life stretches beyond and is richer than the machine!

It must be a person's duty to see to it that outer life never occupies more than half of his existence, the other half welling up from the depth of his self. Man must not become just "the tool of his tools," as H. D. Thoreau warned in *Walden*.[246] Chance and intuition must match the prosaic materialism and create the balanced life. The modern reality perhaps demands that half of a person's life is controlled by spiritless habits, He must however see to it that the other half remains free and unfettered. "A man should be in control of things, rather than allowing things to control him."[247] If all is planned, stiff and angular, he becomes blind to the holiness of life. The outer crude square needs the inner soft circle; otherwise he runs the risk of merely existing and not living. G. Marcel expressed concern about what would become of man if his feeling of sacredness entirely disappeared![248]

As Frieda Fordham says, reflecting Jung, "A man is not a machine who can continually and steadily adapt himself to his environment; he must also be in harmony with himself, that is, adapt to his world within; conversely, he can only adapt to his internal world and achieve harmony with himself when he is adapted to the environmental conditions!"[249] Or

---

[245] N. Berdyaev 1961, p. 35.
[246] H. D. Thoreau 1949, p. 30.
[247] D. J. Munro 1969, p. 152.
[248] In Gabriel Marcel's lecture on 30 November, 1961, at Berkeley.
[249] F. Fordham 1953, p. 19.

as Arthur Koestler puts it, “Machines cannot become like men, but men can become like machines.”[250] Or as Douglas Adams (1952-2001) puts it, “Where there are machines, there are bound to be machine worries, where there are machine worries there are bound to be machine hearts”,[251] and finally Nikolai Berdyaev (1874-1948): “the soul itself agonises helplessly beneath its wheels.”[252]

Man should not end up as a robot or a machine. Machines are valuable for mankind but man is much more so. He is a living organism, capable of *using* the machines!

90. The Doppler Effect of Time

In the Bible it says that man should not worry for more than one day at a time. One shall not care for the morrow. In a true life of insight and intuition one need not worry for even the actual day. This, of course, depends on a number of conditions. A fixed, secure life at the seaside is easy to handle in comparison with the life on the open ocean – in spite of the fact that more people drown at the seashore than in deep water. It is also worth noting that the uncertain future causes more anxiety than the past and the now. This is inevitable for a person who is on the move, and a suitable portion of healthy worry before the battle is necessary for victory. Even so, a person of pragmatic bent should not need to worry as long as his moves are profoundly felt and inspired. He should be as little infected by the future as by the past! He should live fully in the present!

Perhaps it is impossible to live fully in accord with the Bible in this day and age. There must be some planning in private life. Let us say that a day should be exchanged for a year. A sector of life – employment, housing, clothes, and the like – requires this much worrying, but a year should be enough.

---

[250] A. Koestler 1971, p. 251. The comparison of man and machine has a long history. Famous is La Mettrie’s (1709-1751) *L’homme Machine*, “Man the Machine” (1747). See A. Vartanian 1960.

[251] Douglas Adams1979.

[252] N. Berdyaev 1961, p. 82.

91. Money and Minimal Life

Money should not be the aspiration and goal of life. If one's private life is lived in accordance with dictates from within, enough money comes one's way at the proper time. While it may not be so much, it will certainly be enough to live. In this kind of life one is further satisfied with just enough. And with little one is healthier than with much. Do not trouble yourself to get new things! Learn instead to appreciate the old things, and reach for something new when the soul dictates that the appropriate time has come. One is satisfied with one pair of shoes, and one buys a new pair only when the old ones have become sufficiently 'holy'. As Socrates observed, "He is nearest God who need the fewest things."

If one acquires things only in accord with what is deeply felt, there will be things around oneself which reflect sentiment and memory. Haven't we all met people who suffer from property indigestion without being able to savour what they already possess? None of us should forget that everything, in the end, is dust and ashes! With this criterion, one will indeed find many things that can be avoided – and have time for other more valuable things.

The survival of mankind also demands that we learn to economise and go for less. With a world population of about six billion and expected to rise to nine billion we can only expect the global poverty to grow, if Mammon continues to be worshipped and a minority unashamedly hoard millions, even billions of wealth, and the media focus on them and exalt the Golden Calf. The world must learn to economise, minimum rather than maximum should be honoured, and there will be enough for even nine billion people on our globe.

It is also about time that, in this age of affluence, people learn to treasure a few (old) objects rather than succumbing to the urge to add what is not necessary. This will also entail preventing envy to direct purchases. People desire to be alike and are susceptible to what people nearby have acquired. Do we not see house after house virtually identical, possessing the same accoutrements? Commercials play on human weaknesses and seduce people to strive for equal standards.

92. *Coincidentia oppositorum*

If you are open inward, you will also be open outward. This does not need to concern just great things; it can as well concern the most minuscule things. Opposites coincide. There is something strange in the complementarity of opposites, how they contrast and harmonise.

Once one accepts the small thing, one can expect the great thing. Hence, one should never let the slightest thing or humblest person pass by without due respect and love. It is said that there is a greater blessing hidden in the humble thing or person than in all the stars above. While this might be trying for modern science to understand and swallow, yet this is a divine law in life, just as in nature generally.

Nicholas of Kues (1401-1464) calls this law *coincidentia oppositorum.* This was never a secret to the Chinese, who perceived matters generally as complementary pairs. No A without a B and no B without an A. No positive without a negative and no negative without a positive. This equilibrium can easily be discerned both in nature and in life generally. A Russian soldier realised this truth suddenly when digging a trench on the eastern front in 1915: "When you dig down, you dig up." Henry David Thoreau expressed similarly that you must dig down deep in order to aim high.

Neither was it a secret to the Greeks and the Romans. For them all reality was a *coincidentia oppositorum.* In all workings of Destiny, whether in the large order of nature or in the minute order of man, everything was balanced so that every deed, good or evil, had its reverse. The Greek dramas by Aeschylos, Sophocles and Euripedes are built upon this principle. The modern laws of physics, likewise, show the inevitable harmony of opposites. The Roman saying *Contraria sunt complementa*, 'Contraries are complementary', is quoted on the coat of arms of the Danish physicist Niels Bohr. The Destiny of the Greeks and modern physics evince the intuitive communion, universal spontaneity and dynamic order of Creation which harmonise Balance and Perfection.[253]

In *The Tiger's Heart*, H. Howarth portrays *coincidentia oppositorum*, saying that beauty lies in the balancing off and unity of opposites, just as the beauty of art lies in the collation and identity of opposites.[254]

---

[253] See T. Torrance, quoted in J. C. Eccles 1980, pp. 245-246, and A. N. Whitehead 1925, pp. 10-11.

[254] H. Howarth 1970, p. 21.

93. Heraclitus

The ancient Greek philosopher, Heraclitus (ca. 535-475 B.C.), known to us through quotes and fragments in later writings presents the 'opposites' as the Law of the World (logos) determining things and universal harmony. Everything originates from the Eternal, functions in contraries in both the Macrocosm and the Microcosm and are but reflections of each other. All phenomena are linked and contain the germ of their opposites as in the Chinese *yin-yang* image. Through space and time they have this double dimension. The movements are in harmony, and order and meaning pervade them.

This harmony can be observed in every niche of nature. Likewise, it is discerned in social life. Just as there are natural forces there are social forces, and they strive to harmonise. However, they are never static since all things change and move. Society is alive just as Nature is alive, and harmonies 'tilt', as soon as they reach their culmination. "Where nothing ever changes resembles nothing more than the grave."[255]

Heraclitus is mostly remembered for his phrases, "Everything is in a flux (*panta rei*)" and "You cannot step twice into the same river," which summarise his thinking.

94. Voice of Silence

Coincidentia oppositorum reveal the Will operating in the depth of the soul. Life begins inwards and is expressed outwards. It was a mistake by priests and churches, when they turned the eyes of the believers more to the terrestrial world than to the inner psychic world, where the true source of life is found. It was another mistake, born out of religious egoism and conceit, if not out of ignorance, when the route to the happy truth was made difficult and God was confined within four walls. The established religions have made religion seem like something that has to go via temples and popes. The clerics have exploited people's fear of death and hope for deliverance and salvation for their own ambitions. The entrance to the Truth was made narrow and the seeker considered

[255] Quotation from P. E. Firchow 2002, p. 209.

a heretic and even burned at the stake when finding his way without clergy and church.

The inner voice is for all to seek and no cleric or guru is needed. Each human being has his private radar. Woe on all the church institutions and organizations, bishops and popes, who have not only made the entrance narrow but literally placed themselves in the entrance, preventing the seeker to enter without first selling himself. This might seem exaggerated, but the fact is that no one tends to be so self-centred and biased as leaders of religious sects and political parties.[256]

Happiness is for everyone to realise in his own intuitive chamber. A long list of saints prove that it was not the institution that saved a person but he himself within himself. At best, an association or a church served an auxiliary role. Listen, for example, to what St. Augustine (354-430 A.D.) said, following his singular experience:

"Recognise in yourself something within, within yourself. Leave aside the external things (*relinque foris et vestem tuam et carnem tuam*); descend into yourself; go to that hidden apartment, your soul! If you are far from your own self, how can you draw near to God? Not in the body, but in the mind was man made in the image of God. In his likeness let us seek God; in his own image recognise the Creator."[257]

This was the way St. Augustine expounded his experience, fulfilled on his own. It could not be expressed better. If you just exchange 'God' and the 'Creator' for the One, the message is the same in Neo-Platonism.[258] Plotinus' motto for an illuminated life was: "Descend into yourself; go to that secret and hidden apartment, your soul and return to the One, the source from which you came!" "Rejoice in the revelation and nurse your soul! Enter into yourself and attain your imperishable bliss." This inner communion is a route open for all and need not be considered strange and unreachable. Truth one does not find on a mountain peak but within oneself. It is surprising that this message made by Plotinus and the father of all Christians is not heard more loudly in sermons.

---

[256] Cf. *Luke*, 11: 52.

[257] As St. Augustine also says in his *Confessions*, "I entered into my inmost self, thou being my guide. I entered and beheld with the eye of my soul ... the light unchangeable. ... He who knows that light knows eternity. ... Love knows that light." The One equals the *Tao* in Chinese thought.

[258] Cf. "The Lord is One." *Mark*, 12: 29.

95. Meister Eckhart

St. Augustine was not the only Christian to express this inward experience. Every religious age displays their St. Augustines who have experienced the cosmic feeling and interior peace. One meets them East and one meets them West. Any true religion has them. It would be sectarian hubris to deny this fact. Meister Eckhart (ca. 1260-1327) followed in their footsteps, professing that something uncreated and eternal is the soul's essence. He uses the Latin name *scintilla*, 'spark', for this essence and he describes it as spirit and truth in the likeness of God. Meister Eckhart thought of God as an immortal spirit. Mortals cannot exist separated from the spirit – they are in it.

Meister Eckhart advises man to turn inward and seek the Divine Providence in himself, the spark of the divine, his *scintilla*. When he uses the term 'uncreated', he demonstrably refers to the inner half of man, which unites with the other side of phenomena. He also describes this half as the universal soul, the uncreated light, the heavenly melody, that helps man to face each situation in a state of equanimity and detachment.

Meister Eckhart's depiction of the union of the soul with God was coloured with the emphasis on both the transcendence and immanence of the Absolute. What he describes as Being (*Wesen*) sounds close to the *Tao* in Chinese thought. Close to this thinking was Nicholas of Kues with his thought of opposites (*coincidentia oppositorum*) in perfect harmony. One wonders whether other words could conceptualise more fittingly what these thinkers experienced. They have undeserved been accused of 'mysticism' by a later 'rational' world.[259]

One can imagine the *scintilla* as the existential heart where the Temporal and the Eternal converge and where the duality of body and soul ceases to exist. The infinite light can be seen as a wonderful way to describe the Eternal as it replenishes reality and inspires man. For Meister Eckhart all eternity is concentrated in the name of God, which fitted his time, but may be confusing in a later age when God is 'put on a pedestal', beyond and above. In this œuvre the term Eternal is used for Meister Eckhart's God and *scintilla*. Man and Eternity join in the sacred order of light and harmony. The Eternal streams through soul, heart, mind and

---

[259] J. C. Cooper 1981, p. 114.

matter and guides the Whole. This oceanic feeling of oneness with the ultimate reality is a *unio mystica* in which man is free.[260] Facing only outwards, his existence is determined by worldly habits and conventions, and he is unfree.

96. Stoic Thought and Marcus Aurelius

The Stoic philosophy existed for some five hundred years as an organised movement and Zeno of Citium (334-262 B.C.) is considered the founder. Later outstanding figures were Seneca (2 B.C. - 65 A.D.), Epictetus (55-135 A.D.), Cicero (106-43 B.C.) and Marcus Aurelius (121-180 A.D.).

The Stoic ethics has always been found impressive and admirable and the word 'stoic' is in familiar use also in our day with the admiring tone of "withstanding adversity without complaint." Outstanding example is Seneca who, according to tradition, without complaint committed suicide on Emperor Nero's (37-68 A.D.) order.

Stoic philosophy was a natural creed with the Eternal pervading everything. The Eternal becomes, as it were, the self-awareness of Nature and the Whole. It presents a Stoic world of universal law. The creed was rational, showing a realism that recognised also death as an integral part of existence and the companion of life. The Stoic was therefore known to accept life's vicissitudes with dignity, even ending life like Seneca.

Stoicism probably suited the late Greek era and the early Roman empire when men lived short and turbulent lives – not unlike the samurai in medieval Japan.

When reading Marcus Aurelius' *Meditations*, one finds a *Weltanschauung* that comes near to the vision of the Whole. His discourse on 'withdrawing into yourself' leading to tranquillity and just action equals turning inward and experiencing the happy calm of being. When reading "Love only what falls to your lot and is destined for you; what is more suited to you than that?", it is the Stoic gospel in a nutshell.

The Stoic sage and the Taoist sage seem in unison. They share the belief that it is within man's power to achieve happiness and that unhap-

---

[260] The oceanic feeling is apparently not for everyone. Freud complained in 1930 that he could not discover the "oceanic feeling in himself."

piness is the result of pursuing what is not wholly under the control of the individual." If there is a difference, it is the "Stoic" pessimism that runs counter to the Taoist optimism.

97. Plotinus

An early religious philosopher and saintly visionary in the West was Plotinus (ca. 204-270) who belonged to the Platonic tradition. Though he lived in the early Christian era he seems never to have been in touch with Christianity. On the other hand, he is said to have influenced St. Augustine and St. Thomas Aquinas. He was the last great philosopher of antiquity.

Like Plato, Plotinos firmly believed that man's soul was part of a better and higher Whole and he wrote, "I call forth the most glorious life within me, I have become one with the One." Everything radiated from the One, the Absolute, the First Principle. He sensed the complementarity of things and that "reality is neither thought nor thing, but the indissoluble union of thought and thing"[261] – like *yin* and *yang* in Chinese thought. He felt the ubiquity of things: "Every one has all things in himself, so that all things are everywhere, and all is all and each is all, ... and nothing that really is can ever perish."[262]

Plotinus' creed is found in the *Enneads*, compiled by his student Porphyry, and these scriptures express vividly that the world beyond is the true world and this world only an emanation. The One is the 'eternally self-subsisting Unity', a Godhead, from whom all beings derive and maintain identity. He "is not in the world: rather the world is in Him."[263] The aim of such an intuitive life is man's pursuit of freedom from physical hindrances in addition to becoming an integral part of the complexity and richness of things. Man's soul is divine and at death, "the divine in man departs to unite with the Divine of the One."

Plotinus identified a number of ways to attain complete unity with the One. He says, "There are different roads by which the One may be attained: the love of beauty which exalts the poet, the devotion to true

[261] Quotation found in A. Fox 1960, p. 165.
[262] *Enneads*, V. 8,4. Quoted in A. O. Lovejoy 1960, p. 206, and W. R. Inge 1925, p. 381.
[263] A. Fox 1960, p. 164.

knowledge, the love toward others, prayers and contemplation. These lead above the actual and particular to where we stand in the presence of the One who shines out as from the depths of the soul."

Plotinus fits in with the rare saints – East or West. He joins the two greatest Christian philosophers, St. Augustine and St. Thomas Aquinas. He is referred to as "the great thinker who must be, for all time, the classical representative of inner philosophy. No other classical thinker approaches Plotinus in insight and profound penetration."[264]

98. Being – *U* – and Nonbeing – *Mu* – in China

In China one observes a balanced oneness prevalent in religion and philosophy since earliest times. The Whole is comprised of two halves, first *mu*, 'nonbeing' or 'nothingness' and second *u* 'existing' or 'existent'. The *mu*, 'nothing' can be taken as a term which represents the eternal side and pure being, while *u*, 'existent', refers to things in their cosmic *Dasein*. Chinese classics from the earliest times onwards reveal a symmetry of nonbeing *mu* and being *u*, and at no time deny the *mu* reality. *Mu* is always mentioned before *u* and may be compared with Meister Eckhart's 'eternal light', or Jacob Böhme's *Urgrund*, or the 'Eternal Indivisible unity without limit,'[265] or the 'eternal energy' of modern physics. *Mu* contains the 'roots', or 'beginnings' of the *u* side. Whether described as 'light', or 'energy', it is without shape and beyond time and space. Hence, the use of the term *mu*, 'nothingness' is justifiable. It is a 'loaded' nothingness, however, that comprises the 'seeds' of all cosmic shapes and configurations, that is, *u*. The Chinese have the two terms *hsing-chih-shang*, Jap. *keijijô*, 'what is above (without) shapes' (metaphysical), and *hsing-chih-hsia*, Jap. *keijika*, 'what is below (with) shapes' (physi-

---

[264] W. R. Inge, quoted in B. Magee 1998, p. 30.

[265] K. Fischer 2004, pp. 83-88. Or as Böhme says in the *Mysterium Magnum*: "What I consider God is, then, he is the ONE; in reference to the *Creature* an Eternal Nothing. He has neither Foundation, Beginning or Abode ... He is himself only ONE; he needs neither Space or Time ... He is neither like or resembles *any thing* and has no peculiar Place where he dwells." *Ibid.* p. 86. See also R. F. Brown 1977, pp. 54-64 *et passim.*

cal). Form and shape make the difference between what is eternal and what is temporal.

Throughout their long tradition the Chinese embraced a belief in the equilibrium of *mu* and *u*. An early example is Taoism. A later example is *Zen* meditative Buddhism which harmonises with Taoism. Eternity crystallises into temporality. Myth finds expression in ritual. When life flows from the inner transcendent experience, outward reality responds. This is referred to as the life of non-action (*wu-wei*, Jap. *mui*) in Taoism.[266] In Neo-Confucianism, as asserted by Chu Hsi, the same unity is expressed by the Unlimited (*wu-chi*, Jap. *mukyoku*) on the eternal side and the Grand Limited (*t'ai-chi*, Jap. *taikyoku*) on the cosmic side.[267] The Sage, whether Taoist or (Neo-)Confucian, saw things as a seamless whole, an undifferentiated unity of inner and outer.[268]

99. Harmony in Taoism and Confucianism

Both Taoist and Confucian scholars harked back to an idealised past, a Golden Age, when everything was in harmony and man formed a Trinity with Heaven and Earth. Heaven (*t'ien*) represented the transcendent half and Earth the immanent half of reality. Man was located in-between and responsible for their maintenance. He was there to assist Heaven and Earth. The emperor, the Son of Heaven, as Heaven's representative on Earth, had the prime duty in this maintenance. It depended first of all on him whether the Whole was in harmony or not. Heaven was the

---

[266] The *Tao-Te-Ching* and the *Chuang Tzu* are pearls in world philosophy. Chuang Tzu, like Lao Tzu, puts *Tao* above Heaven. It is the Providence that rules from above Heaven. It is the uppermost unnameable Balance (*Tao*). Then follows the cosmic balance, the balance of nature, the balance of the animate world, the balance of the social world and finally the balance of man. All Balances emanate from the same *Tao* and Chuang Tzu uses some twenty terms for this "unnameable" first universal Balance. See, for example, the first chapter of the *Tao-Te-Ching* or the seventh chapter of the *Chuang Tzu*.

[267] Chu Hsi's unity in duality, in which *ch'i*, energy-matter, concurs with *li*, "order-purpose" expresses the union of the two sides. Jacob Böhme was close to the Neo-Confucian *mukyoku* when he spoke of the *Urgrund*, the "Eternal Nothing" of things.

[268] W. T. de Bary, *Neo-Confucian Individualism and Holism*, pp. 338-339, in D. J. Munro 1969.

source of the Way (*Tao*) and rites, rituals, and norms (*li*) were central in what the Way decreed.[269]

All is balanced not only in religion and philosophy but in culture generally. Everything matches as in the imperial dress where design to the left is paired with design to the right!

In classical times the Chinese expressed this harmony with the *yin* and the *yang* (*yin-yang* 陰陽, Jap. *inyô*), the two forces which together compose and animate everything. Through their intercourse all things come into being and all things vanish, including Heaven (which is predominantly *yang*) and Earth (which is predominantly *yin*). *Yin* corresponds to darkness, cold, contraction, the female sex, the valley and river, while *yang* corresponds to light, warmth, expansion, male gender, mountain, sun and fire. They form a duality, a circle in symmetry, and their cyclic movement decides the course of the universe. In the *yin* half there is always a spot of *yang*, and in the *yang* half always a spot of *yin*. The dark always contains an element of light, and vice versa.[270] Jung compares them with animus (*yin*) and anima (*yang*) and A. Koestler refers to them as *sofia*, masculine logic, and *osia*, feminine intuition.[271]

100. Symmetry in Chinese Thought

Both in Taoist and Confucian writings the *ch'i* (*ki*) vital energy-matter gives the world of being a universal dimension. Mencius (372-289 B.C.) laid stress on the *ch'i* 'flood-like energy' that constitutes all reality. In Sung times the *li* (*ri*), laws and forms, was added. The *li* constituted the eternal universal, the rationale of each phenomenon. The *ch'i* and *li*

[269] An approximate comparison would be the Eternal = Heaven, Christ = *Tao* and the Word = *li*.

[270] The *yin* and *yang* thinking might have been developed as early as 1000 B.C., but since it first appears in writing in the fourth century B.C., it cannot with certainty be said what comes from earlier times and what was new interpretations during the great philosophical centuries from the sixth to the third century B.C. In essence, the *yin* and *yang* are Heaven and Earth in other terms. The whole cosmos is seen as an interplay of these two forces, and everything that exists is considered to possess the characteristics of both.

[271] A. Koestler 1960, pp. 281-282.

formed the divine orchestra of harmonious order and established the boundaries for all phenomena and their interaction.[272]

Mencius' *ch'i* thinking was already advanced in Han times and later adopted in Neo-Confucian philosophy, first by Chu Hsi in the *ch'i-li* (*ki-ri*) philosophy and next by Wang Yang-ming (1472-1529) in the *liang chih* (*ryôchi*), 'good knowledge', philosophy.[273] Wang Yang-ming's concentration on the heart (*kokoro*) made him refer to an 'internal lord' (*chu tsai* 主宰, Jap. *shusai*)[274] amidst 'the thousands changes and the ten thousand transformations.' He said that "if there is no 'lord' the *ch'i* will simply run wild." Chu Hsi, too, referred to a "lord" ultimately controlling existence. Questioned, he stated, "Heaven revolves and spreads in all directions. It is now sometimes said that there is a person 'up there' who judges all evil actions; this is assuredly wrong. But to say that there is no ordering [*li*, principle] would be equally wrong." Thus, both Chu Hsi and Wang Yang-ming did not see this 'lord' outside man's heart and mind as a godhead above. It was not an anthropomorphic God but rather an anthropopathic essence, called a *sensorium* by Newton.[275] Neither went outside the human heart to realise identity with the divine. For all of them internal conceptions inspired external perceptions.[276]

The traditional Chinese thinkers would consider the rise of science one-sided, as it forsakes the harmonious relationship between the celestial dimension (Heaven) and the physical dimension (Earth). While the West has cloven the Whole into bits and pieces, the Chinese have never left the Whole out of sight – and, as a result, come behind in technical knowing.

"Nothing endures save the flow of energy and the rational order that pervades it," words by Thomas Henry Huxley (1825-1895) with which Chu Hsi, Wang Yang-ming and Einstein would agree.

---

[272] Heaven and Earth are the parents of all creation, says Chuang Tzu. Jung calls *ch'i*, "the world stuff," and *li* the "world soul."

[273] Chu Hsi was the pivot of the Neo-Confucian thought. He matched inner self-cultivation with outer study of things and social concern, emphasizing both observation and intuition. Wang Yang-ming stressed intuition.

[274] Synonymous with *chen tsai* 真宰 , Jap. *shinsai*, "true lord", *Chuang Tzu*, ch. 2.

[275] J. Gleick 2004, p. 192. *Sensorium*, an inner organ for divine perception.

[276] The Greek physician Galen (ca. 130-200) recognised that nature has an inner purpose and often uses an object for more than one purpose. He endorsed experimental physiology.

101. Søren Kierkegaard (1813-1855) and Either-Or

An uncompromising attitude, an all-or-nothing mentality, is manifested in Søren Kierkegaard's *Either-Or*.[277] From a strictly Christian point of view Kierkegaard was correct. It is an Either or an Or! This is symptomatic of Christian fundamentalism: God or the World. Each new sect has decried the earthly reality and demanded more faith in God – usually meaning the specific God of the sect! A generous *Both-And* as in eastern philosophies and religions is usually not accepted.[278]

In the West the faithful perceive a chasm between what is Good and Bad – between Heaven and hell. Significantly, there is no such clear separation of Good and Bad in the East, where a speck of evil is found in what is good and a speck of good in what is evil and where the entirety spells truth.

In Kierkegaard's works one also meets the dimension of living religion versus institutional religion. Christ's kingdom of Heaven has hardened into a church on earth. Clergy had come to dominate Christianity – in cooperation with a state machinery and officialdom! Kierkegaard emphasised that Christ demanded that the private person alone pursue the quest of the Infinite; the "big leap" rests with him.[279]

102. India

In India one encounters such a richness of religion, in fact, so rich and varied that the rest of the globe seems spiritually poor. As an Indian politician stated not long ago, "Religion we have in such surplus that we can export it." Indians have religion enough for export, and the secularised westerner turns more and more to India in his quest of religious truth. He only runs the risk of losing himself among the wealth of detail from

---

[277] Kierkegaard's *Either-Or* is best presented in the *Øieblikket*, "the Moment" (1854-55).

[278] See, for example, H. Kochanek (ed.) 1998, pp. 30-42.

[279] Kierkegaard's "big leap" can, *mutatis mutandum*, be compared with Nicholas of Kues' *De docta ignorantia* and Christ's statement that only as a child can you enter the Kingdom of God. Religious life was the great "paradox" – something that it had not been in earlier ages.

the start and never reach the core of Indian piety, which is plain and simple. The fact is that once all the frills are gone, the sacred view is easy to comprehend. Again one has the basic equilibrium of the eternal and temporal. There is *Brahman*, the universal soul, on the eternal side, and *Atman*, the individual soul, on the temporal side. The tradition has remained the same since the time of the Vedas. Sacrifice and self-mortification are mentioned in those early hymns and have been important ever since.

In Hinduism the basic truth is expressed in the simple three-word phrase: *Tat Tvam Asi*, 'Thou art That.' *Tat* stands for the Unknowable [Creator] (*Brahman*) and is identical with you. There is no duality, only a holy monism, the All in the One. Man descends into himself where *Brahman* dwells and constitutes his *atman*, his soul or self. Hence, his *atman* is not only divine but also identical with the Eternal and each person joins all others as a jewel on the Indra's net of essential being. The *Tat Tvam Asi* unites men and women as brothers and sisters and thereupon relates to all Creation, whether animal, tree or rock. "The entire universe is permeated with the same soul stuff that each one of us bears within."[280] The world is an illusion, described as a delusive 'appearance' or as a 'shadow play without even a play.'[281] *Brahman* "dwells in the lotus of every heart", and in meditation one senses a hidden internal relation with the numinous essence of the All. Buddhism, in all its appearances, is an outgrowth of Hindu spirituality. It proclaims the oceanic feeling of oneness with the entire universe and the unity of the Buddha soul in all beings. Its simple message declares that life is suffering and that man should strive for *nirvana*, that is, freedom from endless reincarnations and delusions.[282]

Where the Indians go far is in striving for enlightenment – so far as to negate mundane life. The same obsession with the attainment of illumination can be discerned among orthodox believers in other religions. One encounters extreme elements and groups in all creed. Perhaps the momentum and energy of the psyche demand a total engagement in whatever creed one embraces. At first glance, it seems that the concen-

---

[280] See A. C. Danto 1972, p. 38.
[281] C. Eliot 1921, I: 45.
[282] This has invited the allegation that the Hindu and the Buddhist are rather agnostic than religious.

tration is overly inward, and that the demand for religious devotion and asceticism goes too far. Now, a healthy inner life asks for a healthy outer life, and any over-emphasis on either is detrimental to sound human life.

In the Persian (Muslim) Sufism we meet a doctrine that is of a piece with Hindu and world-embracing inspirational thought. Its well-known poet Jalaluddin Rumi (1207-1273) puts the creed simply:

> I know nothing of two worlds
> all I know is the One
> I seek only One,
> I know only One,
> I find only One.

103. India, China and Japan

The Chinese have never seen any cosmogony running through Creation. There has never been a beginning, nor has there ever been a goal of Creation. There has been no need to subdue nature like in the West. The tendency in Chinese thought has been dialectic, moving like waves from harmony to harmony, from dynasty to dynasty. In similar fashion, the Indians have seen a perpetual, dynamic process of becoming. The cycle of birth, death and rebirth is for the Indian as natural as the seasons which occur and recur in an unending fashion. Liberation from the wheel of life and death can only be achieved in union with *Brahman* according to Hinduism and through Nirvana according to Buddhism. Both the Indians and the Chinese have been religious throughout history but without any apparent attachment to institution, doctrine or godhead. Likewise, the Japanese have mixed their creeds, without losing their souls. All three have taken the message so naturally that they can declare themselves to be gnostics and agnostics on the same day. Religion has been more a matter of natural life than a matter of lofty thought. The Oneness of the Whole has been the innate awareness in the East, equalling the same in Greek thought and proto-science.

In Hinduism everything is holy and manifested in each man and woman. Man's soul is not separated from the universal soul, but joined in kind with the Eternal. This is different from Christianity where the human soul joins the universal soul in the hereafter. In the Hindu religion the Eternal rests everlastingly in man's soul; he comes from the Eternal, lives in the Eternal and ends up in the Eternal. Every individual is free to seek enlightenment without the help of a cult or a prophet.

The Hindu would say that he knows and lives his divine light. He feels in the middle of the universe that is tuned to a cosmic harmony. Like the Buddhist, Taoist and Confucian he is not a theist. They all have their myths and ritual observances but ancestors are more honoured and worshipped than prophets and gods. Their creeds are emanations of the Eternal and cannot be rationalised, intellectualised and explained. They are feeling pure and indeterminate, leading to "the great spirit of the universe that informs everything that has life."[283]

The Japanese Shintoism recognises a cosmogony, and has gods, myriads of them, and a Sun Goddess who tops them all, but, basically, it is an all-embracing animism and vitalism, which sees divinity (*kami*) in all things, also in man.

104. *Zen*, Natsume Sôseki and *Satori*

One author who presents a good picture of the modern seeker and the closed access to the higher truth is the Japanese laureate Natsume Sôseki (1867-1916). In the novel under the title *Mon*, 'Gate', the hero Sosuke goes to a *Zen* temple to do *zazen*. One of the heart-breaking passages in modern literature is the description of his defeat:

> He had come to the gate (*mon*) and had asked to have it opened. The bar was on the other side and when he knocked, no one came. Then a voice is heard saying: "Knocking will do no good. Open it yourself." He stood there and asked himself how he could open it. He thought of a plan, but he could not find the strength to put it into effect. ... He lacked the courage to go back. He then looked at the great gate which would never open for him. He was never intended to pass through it. Nor was he meant to be content until he was allowed to do so. He was, then, one of the those unfortunate beings who must stand by the gate, unable to move, and patiently wait for the day to end.

The predicament of most people today is allegorised in this passage. They hear of the gate, face the gate, and then a voice states tersely, "Knocking is no good. Open it yourself." The poor seeker stands there

[283] Quotation in F. S. C. Northrop 1946, p. 404.

wondering how he could possibly open it, but lacks the courage to do so. He concludes sadly that he is not predestined to pass through.

This allegory, written in 1910, is certainly put in a *Zen* setting but it could easily illustrate the situation in other religions. Natsume Sôseki was possibly affected by a long stay in the West.

This calls to mind an encounter with *Zen* monks on a train from Tokyo to Osaka. In a lively conversation they were asked whether they had achieved '*satori*', or 'enlightenment'. All of them answered in chorus and unhesitatingly, "Oh, no! We have been monks for only fifteen years, we have yet a long way to go. '*Satori*' takes long to realize." Whereupon, they pulled out their *santori* whisky flasks from the pockets of their gowns and took a gulp.

If even monks who spend fifteens years in a temple cell cannot manage the 'gate', one should not be surprised that a Sosuke gives up when only approaching the awesome 'gate'. How sad that this 'gate' is made so difficult to enter that monks after fifteen years give up and rather turn to whisky! Ironically, indicative of this age, the whisky becomes the surrogate 'gate.'[284]

105. Franz Kafka and other Modernists

Modern European literature gives expression to a similar pessimism. Franz Kafka (1883-1924) is probably the most well known writer who has given expression of this sentiment in his novels. In *Das Schloss* ('The Castle', written in 1920) the hero makes desperate efforts to gain access to "the castle", that dark, mysterious other world for which he longs. He struggles in vain but never manages to penetrate its mysterious within. He remains an eternal stranger in the world into which he is

[284] In life there are as many keyholes and keys as there are people. One thing they share: everyone must open his own private "gate." He must turn the gaze inward and find the way to what a Hindu would call the "lotus of his heart." What is often overlooked is that "gates" like "walls" can be by-passed and "overcome." People forget that one does not fight locked doors or walls. In religion just as in life generally one must learn to overcome obstacles, just as an army circumvents an enemy fortress. On the other side new radiant panoramas will open up.

"thrown" and cut off from true reality.[285] In *Der Prozess* ('The Trial', written in 1914) the hero is lost in the entanglements of a legal process, he loses his self and ends up being executed. This human wretchedness is also vividly described by Rainer Maria Rilke in his poem 'The Great Night'. Rilke (1875-1926) voices his sentiments about "the big city inaccessible", and he finds himself a stranger locked out and ALONE "exposed on the mountains of his heart." He portrays the decadence of the West and the forlornness and angst in the big city culture where the depersonalised modern man loses contact with the divine, feels homeless and even prefers death to life.[286]

A modern Japanese writer, Abe Kôbô, describes the same existential dilemma in his novel *Suna no onna*, ('The Woman in the Dunes', written in 1968). The hero is trapped in a hole in a desert with sand all around. At first he struggles for a way out but then resigns to his fate and attains his peace, finding contentment with a woman and water-making.

Jean Paul Sartre, the atheistic-nihilistic existentialist, has described man's tragic condition in a world devoid of absolute values in *La Nausée* (1983). As a substitute value he recommends political activity in works, such as *Hui clos* (1944) and *Les mains sale* (1948). Albert Camus is close to the same existential nausea in the face of the 'absurdity of existence' in *L'Etranger* (1942) and *La Peste* (1948).

One can sense the same gloom in modern poetry, for example, in the works of Charles Baudelaire (1821-1867), Arthur Rimbaud and Paul Verlaine (1844-1896). When Verlaine penned the words, 'Il pleure dans mon cœur comme il pleure dans la ville' ('it rains in my heart just as it rains in the city'), he articulated what can easily be felt in much contemporary poetry. The poet has erred into a tragic impasse and does not know his way out.

In art Edvard Munch (1863-1944) personifies the modern pessimism better than Fjodor Dostoevsky (1821-1881) or Schopenhauer with his picture 'The Scream' (1893) whose "anguished skeletal figure with a

---

[285] Samuel Beckett (1906-1989) expresses the same gloom in dramas such as *Waiting for Godot* (1952).

[286] The illness of existential despair may be traced to the nineteenth century, not earlier, in the West, not in the East. Why? Was it true (psychic) illness or just fashion? Was it due to the *Zeitgeist* or to vanity? In Russia, in Dostoevsky's case, it was quite clearly illness but in Tolstoy's case rather vanity.

mouth frozen in a rictus of psychic pain embodies the existentialist horror, angst and despair."[287] He depicts the anguish of his own soul but next the existential angst of the whole age.

Existential philosophers, for example Martin Heidegger (1889-1976), made attempts to sacralise some aspect of the black mood. If they succeeded is a moot question. Karl Jaspers (1883-1969) seems to have been close to Kierkegaard's words that "you are not a human being without God" in his discussions about 'Grenzsituationen', but he does not mention any Kierkegaardian 'big leap'.

106. Religion and Elation

The aesthetic pleasure of a great piece of art can also evoke religious emotion. Both poetry and music can be bridges which connect the universal soul and the fullest life. You listen to Beethoven's 5th symphony and you are transported beyond the terrestrial world, feeling an inner peace that reaches to your very last cell, and "you know that 'es einen Gott im Himmel gibt'" (Einstein). The same overtone of the infinite is experienced when reading William Wordsworth (1770-1850) in the *Tintern Abbey*:

> While with an eye made quiet by the power
> Of harmony, and the deep power of joy,
> We see into the life of things ...
>
> I have felt
> A Presence that disturbs me with the joy
> Of elevated thoughts; a sense sublime
> Of something far more deeply interfused,
> Whose dwelling is the light of setting suns,
> And the round ocean and the living air,
> And the blue sky, and in the mind of man.[288]

Not only artistic and poetic happenings, however, may cause exhilaration in one's soul. Any great elation, one's first love, a great success, a scenery in nature, recovery from an illness, a moment of passion, a sci-

---

[287] Sarah Lyell in International Herald Tribune, 11-12 February, 2006.

[288] W. Wordsworth, *Lines composed a few miles above Tintern Abbey*, l. 37 and l. 88.

entific insight and other shattering experiences bring the other side into a person's life. As Einstein puts it, "All religions, arts and sciences are branches on the same tree." All things considered, the person is rare who has not felt the immense joy when the eye "in a fine frenzy rolling, doth glance from heaven to earth, from earth to heaven" (Shakespeare, *A Midsummer Night's Dream*). These euphoric occurrences have in common that they come from without, whereas the soul's rapture comes from within.[289] They can be referred to as other-centred religious experiences in contrast to inner-centred religious experiences. It can be argued whether Heaven or Earth should be the beginning of the sublime encounter. Probably Shakespeare is correct when he speaks about "a fine frenzy rolling from Heaven to Earth, from Earth to Heaven," allowing for both the inner and the outer to be the source of blessedness.[290]

107. Man's Boundless Imagination

Once the cobwebs are brushed away from both imagining and reasoning, one finds the source and fount of all original ideas: the inner inspiration. Descartes began there in his logical reasoning, and so does everyone. All things, according to the Bible, are 'vanity of vanities', but the elation in one's soul and heart, radiant in the calm state of peace, is not.

Man's fantasy and imagination are boundless, as boundless as the infinity they attempt to embrace. Often they lose themselves in figments of castles in the air, but truth is hidden in them. Careful study of the endless streams of oral traditions, legends and sagas, that emerge from, for example, the Indian, Chinese, Japanese, Hebrew, Greek power of imagination, display colourful and rich human efforts to depict what in the end defies depiction. What they have in common is that they regard this world as a mere appearance of another unseen aspect of reality. The myths allegorise what surrounds man and justifies his existence, about gods, origin of mankind, death and ancestors. Anthropologists have rich

---

289 F. C. Happold 1963, p. 93, and N. M. Wildiers 1968, p. 117.

290 Communion with nature is recommended by H. D. Thoreau and R. W. Emerson as a way of spiritual life. Others have sought freedom in moral insights and in creative activities. Walt Whitman finds his "soul" in poetry. C. R. Metzger 1961, p. 19.

and endless fields of legends and folklore to interpret. They recognise that all these narratives are attempts to present and describe divine sentiments and encounters. Let's not forget what Hamlet said to Horatio: "There are more things in Heaven and Earth, Horatio, than are dreamt of in your philosophy."[291]

Human curiosity and enquiry is behind religion and philosophy not less than scientific rationalism. Without them, actually, man would be poor and development would be rare or non-existent. "He wants to hear truths which broaden rather than restrict him, which do not obscure but enlighten."[292] He is enriched with myth and culture and he needs both for his equipoise; with only either he is without the joyous equilibrium that a rich and happy life requires. He needs *mythos* for his inner subjective life and *logos* for his outer objective life. Together they widen and complement his horizons.

108. Dr. Sarvepalli Radhakrishnan

Dr. Sarvepalli Radhakrishnan (1888-1975), former president of the Republic of India, had something to say about cobwebs in his conversation with Dom Aelred Graham:[293]

> The hippies and the Beatles! "Transcendental Meditation", as it is called! You see, if you open a classic on yoga, it only tells you that man is full of discord. His heart goes one way; his mind goes another. You should try to bring both, and everything else, harmoniously together. Yoga is merely the method by which you examine yourself every day for a few minutes. Investigate your own nature and sensory input and ask yourself the question: "How can I harmonize the different sides of my nature and make the outward and the inward coincide?" That's the sublime purpose of yoga as you find it in the classical books. For example, the Yoga Sutra begins like that. It tells you that your soul, heart, mind and body are predestined to harmonize. That's the meaning of yoga – not the sort of thing that's happening today. ... Or take the word "*Zen*"; it is the equivalent of *dhyana*, a Sanskrit term meaning "meditation." It merely tells you that you have to penetrate beyond your brain and mind; you have to concentrate deeply until you are

[291] W. H. Thorpe paraphrases in *Biology, Psychology and Belief* (1961), p. 58: "There are stranger things in heaven and earth than are dreamt of in any of our philosophies."

[292] C. G. Jung and R. Wilhelm 1962, p. 143. Adapted.

[293] D. A. Graham 1971, pp. 140-141.

able to realise that celestial radiance, or "suchness" or "thusness", or whatever you would call the sanctuary of your soul. If you are able to accomplish that and allow it to penetrate every cell of your body, then you are an integrated and harmonized individual and enjoy good health. To become integrated involves persistent practice; it's not by mere talk, by chanting mantras and hymns, but by self-examination and submission to the Will. That is what is essential to develop in living. All things considered, the function of religion is the total integration of the personality. Let your depth penetrate to your surface; then the two will coincide.

Dr. Radhakrishnan cuts through the fog of pious practices and takes direct aim at the plain facts of life and religion. He more or less says that the truth is stored in the mysterious room within, where we have to 'inscend' and let intuition colour our lives. The meditative technique is simple and must not be obfuscated with doctrinal demands for seeking the truth that, after all, cannot be attained intellectually.[294]

109. Simplicity is Truth

Truth dwells in simplicity. As the Latin expression says: 'Simplicity is the seal of truth' (*Simplex sigillum veri*). Long and convoluted terminology is no more a sign of truth than are metaphysical systems which attempt to arrive at eternity rationally. Man possesses the ability to complicate truth, and make it impossible for the majority to comprehend it. The fact is, however, that "Everyone longs for simple truths which speak not to the head alone but also to the heart, which bring clarity to the contemplative spirit and peace to the restless pressure of the feelings."[295]

The happy life should not be for the privileged few. Even though everyone is different, everyone has the potential for a happy life. "You know simple life has its grandeur,"[296] says Brecht. And André Comte-Sponville says, "Simplicity is freedom, buoyancy, transparency. As simple as the air, as free as the air ... The simple person does not take himself too seriously or too tragically. ... He goes on his merry way, his heart light, his soul at peace. ... The world is his kingdom ... and the present his eter-

[294] As a comparative philosopher S. Radhakrishnan recognises the unity of all religions and philosophies.

[295] C. G. Jung 1995, p. 46. Adapted.

[296] Bertolt Brecht in *Rise and Fall of the City of Mahagonny*, 1st act.

nity. He has nothing to prove, since he has no appearances to keep up, and nothing to seek, since everything is before him. What is more simple than simplicity? ... It is the life without exaggerations, without lies. ... It is the insignificant life, it is the truth."[297]

"Having a simple mind is not the same as being simple-minded. ... It involves simplifying our acts, our speech and our thoughts and ridding ourselves of the superfluous." It results in clarity of thought and in the freedom from covetousness and vanity. Remember that "It is life near the bone that is sweetest."[298]

Renunciation comes naturally in a life that seeks simplicity. What is not needed, is superfluous and "superfluous wealth can buy superfluities only."[299] Renunciation therefore means freedom from striving, worries and attachment. Being free means to follow the path of innerness and be one's true self; one's happiness increases and anxiety is gone. The baby is the naked ideal. Anyone can return to the spontaneity, innocence and simplicity of the child and realise his authentic self and happiness![300] As Chuang Tzu says, "he who maintains his simplicity is unblended with anything" and "he who embodies simplicity and pristine health is *Tao*'s man." He says further that "he who humbles himself wins hearts."[301] The Taoist Chinese held the "uncarved block" (*p'u*)[302] as the ideal. The raw, uncarved *p'u* is a metaphor for simplicity and fullness. "Be clumsy, it helps", is their useful motto. The haphazard method usually leads to success; in similar fashion, it leads to directness and artlessness. Simplicity reigns the holy! As the philosopher Henry David Thoreau exclaimed: "Our life is frittered away by detail ... Simplify, simplify!"[303]

---

[297] A. Comte-Sponville is quoted in M. Ricard 2006, pp. 165-166. See A. Comte-Sponville 1995, pp. 199-208.

[298] M. Ricard 2006, pp. 164-165, and H. D. Thoreau 1949, p. 218.

[299] H. D. Thoreau 1949, p. 218.

[300] See the Bible and K. Jaspers 1954, pp. 9-10. Remember that "Children and fools tell the truth."

[301] *Chuang Tzu*, ch. 14 and 29.

[302] "Uncarved block" is Arthur Waley's translation of *p'u* in his *The Way and its Power*. The Confucian philosopher Mencius also praised the simplicity of the child. He said, "The great man is he who does not lose his child's heart", *Mêng Tzu* IV: B, 12, 1.

[303] His *Walden* is a eulogy to the simple life.

Or as Confucius put it, "Dressed in a tattered robe quilted with hemp, yet standing by the side of men dressed in furs, and not ashamed; – ah! it is Yu who is equal to this. He dislikes none, he courts nothing![304]

110. The Way of Balance is for Everyone

It is our duty to make the inward divine order accessible to everyone. If we have managed to establish democracy otherwise, why should we not in this respect? The path to the depths of existence should be wide-open for all and lead us to the shores of the Eternal and to the great joy and serenity.[305] The obstacles should be removed so that each person, who wishes, can by his own effort attain the great peace. It should be kept in mind that the inner communion is a private matter; it begins with and ends in personal experience.

We are different both in kind and degree – just as our faces –, and as there are physical differences there are necessarily psychic differences. But the general structure is the same and we all participate in a universal soul. It is reasonable, therefore, to conclude that the avenue leading to the complete person is the same for everybody but that everyone must walk this road in his own individual way. To reach the true goal, however, one must forgo the blinkers of sectarian blindness.

111. Faith, Reason and Order

Faith and reason have been opposites ever since monotheism became prevalent. In polytheistic religions this schism seems never to occur. Originally there was no divide between them in Christian thought either. When Paulus wrote about faith, works and grace, they were not put

---

[304] *Lun Yü* IX: 26. Yu was one of Confucius' loved students. Mahatma Gandhi (1869-1948) similarly stressed that the "standard of living should be limited to the absolute limited." See, for example, E. Stanley Jones 1949, p. 129f.

[305] As Henry Vaughan (1622-1695) puts it in his poetry, "I saw Eternity the other night, like a great *Ring* of pure and endless light, all calm, as it was bright and round beneath it, Time in hours, days, years Driv'n by the spheres Like a vast shadow mov'd, In which the world And all her train were hurled. ..." Quoted in J. Hayward 1956, p. 123.

in separate compartments. A gulf arose in western thinking when faith capitulated to the intellect. Faith has afterwards been up to the individual and Kierkegaard, for one, described it as the "big leap" when turning from reason to faith.[306]

It was an intellectual ambition until Isaac Newton (1642-1727) to reconcile science and religion and to see the unity of faith and reason. Newton considered himself to be God's servant whose duty it was to decipher the laws of God's Creation. He regarded his discoveries as only stations on the way to human understanding of the divine order. Also scientists before him, such as Nicolaus Copernicus (1473-1543) and Johannes Kepler (1571-1630), considered their investigations to be a religious calling. So did others during the following centuries of rationalism and empiricism.[307]

In modern philosophy A. North Whitehead comes close to Newton in his 'philosophy of organism'. The Eternal is the metaphysical energy that exists continuously and ubiquitously, covertly guiding the emergence of molecules from atoms, living organisms from molecules and mind from matter. The universe is an interacting set of events or an evolving process. Religion and science are intrinsically compatible – together comprehended as 'THE ORDER.'[308]

Order is, in truth, the common denominator that links inner and outer thought, East and West. As Whitehead says:

> There is an actual world because there is order in nature. If there were no order, there would be no world. Also since it is a world, we know that there is an order. The ordering and refining entity is a necessary element in the supernatural situation presented by the actual world.

---

[306] What Kierkegaard could recommend was "deep introspection, penetrating through the layers of unconscious distortions to reach, with Böhme, ... spiritual harmony." L. L. Whyte 1979, p. 146.

[307] C. G. Jung concludes, "How on earth do people know that the only reality is the physical atom, when this cannot be proved to exist at all except by means of the psyche? If there is anything which can be described as primary, it must be the psyche, certainly not in any circumstances the atom, which, like everything else in our experience, is only directly given as a model or picture." Jung is quoted in J. W. Krutch 1953, p. 122.

[308] See J. C. Eccles 1980, pp. 244-247, and A. N. Whitehead 1925, p. 3-18. Order is capitalised for emphasis. "Intelligent Design" is today a popular synonym.

T. Jefferson said that, when looking at the Creation with its ORDER, harmony, beauty and wonderful design, one cannot help recognizing a Creator behind it. The divine Will could be learned from observation itself. He wrote to his friend John Adams in 1823: "When we take a view of the universe, in its parts, general or particular, it is impossible for the human mind not to perceive and feel a conviction of DESIGN, consummate skill, and indefinite *élan* in every atom of its composition. ... It is impossible, I say, for the human mind not to believe, that there is in all this, DESIGN, cause and effect, up to an ultimate cause, a Fabricator of all things from matter and motion, their Preserver and Regulator while permitted to exist in their current forms, and their regeneration into new and other forms. We see, too, evident proofs of the necessity of a superintending power, to maintain the universe in its COURSE and ORDER. So irresistible are the evidences of the existence of an intelligent and powerful Agent, that, of the infinite members of men who have existed through time, they have believed in the hypothesis of an eternal Creator, rather than in a self-existent universe. ..."[309] (Emphasis added)

Likewise, the German Romantic philosophers, Friedrich Schelling (1775-1854) among them, expressed that the immediate realization was connected with an inner light and a feeling of being in accord with the ongoing process of nature. All life was a creation of nature beginning and ending with a Creator.

Religion and science find each other in the order of nature. W. Heisenberg expressed that values must be related to a central order and "if this central order should ever become extinguished, terrible things may happen to mankind, far more terrible even than concentration camps and atomic bombs."[310] The Chinese philosopher Wang Yang-ming expressed the same: "If there is no order, the *ch'i* (energy-matter) will simply run wild."[311] Other eminent scholars, for example, Albert Einstein

[309] See E. T. Martin 1952, pp. 125-126. The great scientists, for example Kepler and Newton at the beginning of the modern age and Albert Einstein and Werner Heisenberg in our age, have given expression to the inner feeling in the face of the wondrous harmony and order of the Whole. See B. Lovell 1981, pp. 192-204.

[310] Heisenberg quoted in J. C. Eccles 1980, p. 245, and in J. C. Eccles and D. N. Robinson 1984, p. 76: "What is a soul without wings?"

[311] Wang Yang-ming is quoted in T. A. Metzger 1977, p. 70.

and Max Planck (1858-1947), agree with them.[312] Max Planck concluded that the laws of physics awoke the wondrous impression "that nature was ruled by an rational and purpose-conscious Will (*von einem vernünftigen, zweckbewussten Willen regiert wurde*)."[313]

112. Creeds, Meditation and Prayer

Whoever wishes to bolster up his subjective life with religious faith can anchor it in a religion that suits him. There are many creeds to choose among. As most people need a pillar of life, it is rather recommended that each person turns to the religious practise that is close to his personality. Some *mantra*, contemplation and prayer are essential in life. Our hearts require the imaginary flourishes, the poetic phrases, the sublime music and the "ah-ness" in all living. To be just rational and factual makes man poor.

These practises must come second. First comes the self-realization. When the moving inward has taken place and the tranquil soul is attained, it does not matter whether one uses the one or the other expression, whether one believes in one or another God or whether one has faith in a *samsara* wheel or reincarnation or whether one attends one church or another. One develops a firm belief that all creeds are built on the same base and that every living being is precious and belongs to the same reality. It is not a matter of being a believer, just a matter of being open to one's inner.

113. Symbols and Metaphors

Much can be said about the symbols found in religions. In order to find and maintain inner peace a 'higher object' can be a great help. Symbols such as the cross of the Christian religion and the Buddha figure in Bud-

---

[312] In our day leading physicists generally distance themselves from mechanistic materialism. Both Niels Bohr and Werner Heisenberg have expressed that man is not just an objective observer but a subjective participant in the play of life and nature.

[313] M. Planck 1944, p. 302. In lecture with the title, *Religion und Naturwissenschaft*.

dhism serve this purpose for millions of people. The totem pole serves the same purpose. Also more abstract symbols like the *yin* and *yang* in Chinese philosophy and the *mandala* in Buddhism can help man to preserve a poised heart.

Indeed, for the man at peace with himself, anything can be a cross or an icon. He sees beauty and symmetry everywhere. As Meister Eckhart once said: "We ought to understand God equally in all things for God is equally in all things." The sunny morning brings fuel to the happy mind just as much as the gloomy evening does with its rain and mist. The screechy sound adds to the peace of mind as does the melodious song. The sour taste in the mouth and the rough sensation under the finger tips can produce the same effect. On the other hand, even the most pleasing melody nor the sunniest day will help when one's mind is upset. Even the most radiant day and the most perfect system smacks of hell when the heart is in an uproar and harmony is gone.[314] A stormy day and an imperfect social system can be endured as long as one has the consolation of genuine inner peace.

Generally, when the inside is in order, we find order in the outside, too. On the other hand, when the soul is in disorder, one tends to perceive chaos everywhere. A split mind is split and splits. It is symptomatic of our times, that much is said about chaos not least by existential philosophers. This indicates more the chaos of their minds than that of the world. The person in Balance rather sees order, meaning and harmony even when the world is out of joint – and acts constructively.

114. The Wholesome Feeling of Peace of Mind

The wholesome feeling of Peace of Mind is the prime clue revealing that a person has attained his Balance. It makes its presence felt in many ways. Not self-assertive and arrogant, he is one with himself, free to take things and circumstances as they come. In '*Karain: A Memory*' Joseph Conrad writes:

---

[314] "A heart that is distant creates a wilderness round it," says the Chinese poet T'ao Ch'ien.

> To him who does not come to teach or to rule, to him who asks for nothing and welcomes all things, words are spoken by the camp-fires, in the shared solitude of the sea, in riverside villages, in resting-places surrounded by forests – words are spoken that take no account of race or colour. One heart speaks – another listens; and the earth, the sea, the sky, the passing wind and the stirring leaf, – they all listen also to the futile tale of the burden of life.[315]

Conrad depicts the sentiments of a person who has attained his peace of mind. He acts with kindness and spontaneity and places the other person in the centre, he listens first and speaks afterwards. On the other hand, it is an indication of someone who has not achieved his peace that he loves to teach and be the leader of the pack. This refers particularly to the person, whose heart is a closed circle and who does not exhibit openness toward others. The generous heart is the emblem of the mature person, who has accomplished his equilibrium and attained the clarity of his soul. He is happy "to sit down quietly before whoever comes his way, to observe with interest, to respond and felicitate."[316]

In the fifth century B.C., Confucius said similarly: "The superior man is not absolutely for or against anything in the world. He supports only what is right." The Confucian Middle Way illustrates the complete man, the *chün tzu* 君子, (Jap. *kunshi*), 'noble man', whose conduct is unselfish, just and kind. Another close parallel is found in the *Bhagavad-Gita*: "He who craves for nothing, who is clever and impartial, and has risen above all distractions, who renounces the feeling of doership in all undertakings – that devotee is dear to me."[317]

115. Social Rules and Inner Life

It has been normal to connect ethical rules with religion and to afford them a divine colouring. Hence, they have been regarded as conferred by God or Heaven. The threat of the doom and gloom or a lower reincarnation have helped to make people try to live a decent life. The best thing would be if people would continue to anchor their behaviour in devout beliefs and look forward to unending punishment for acting badly.

---

[315] In J. Conrad 1898, p. 40.
[316] *Ibid.*
[317] *Bhagavad-Gita*, ch. XII.

Once the Eternal is denied, the reason for sin is gone and once the sense of sin is gone, only shame remains.

As the sense of the sacred is lost, cultural norms become the moral rules. Most rules of deportment reflect man's attempts to regularise the flux of change. For example, most traffic regulations reflect the economic situation, created together with the motorcar, and how do you connect driving on the wrong side of the road with God or Heaven? Before the motorcar, they did not exist, and when the motor-car vanishes, they will also vanish. They are practical and set up in accord with the common good and social, political and economic factors and as such in line with divine knowledge.

Ethical rules have traditionally been central to religious life. In China it was Heaven's *Tao* that conferred the practice of rites and rituals and in Greece it was Destiny that directed nature and life. Religious notions were the backbone of justice. The close relationship between the supernatural and the natural has also been evident in western law. Early law was divine grace. Today the law has become secular and the norms are not sacred, but ordained as society demands.

Now, morality is designed for a particular society; it is public and devised so that people can live together. Individuality is private, and it lends quality and colour to otherwise cold and impersonal laws. All wordly doings can be endowed with compassion and can be regarded as 'rites' or 'rituals' as in Confucian thought.

116. Affluence and Poverty

Freedom is as little as half enjoyed when other-determined. Without interior guidance, exterior liberty remains incomplete. The same applies to wealth. The advanced West has brought about unimaginable material affluence, yet the people are as unhappy as ever. Mortals are born who have more than they need but are embattled against themselves. This serves as evidence that happiness is not proportional to wealth. Suicide statistics affirm that there are rather more suicides than earlier when our societies were poor and most people were destitute. It is our present task to create inner freedom as successfully as we have created outer freedom. Once inner freedom is substantiated as much as outer freedom, destructive emotions will potentially be reduced and dissipate.

True liberty is rooted in the inner of the soul. Worldly freedom, however civilised, is only partial as long as the heart is neglected. N. Berdyaev says that the "completely socialized and rationalized man may be entirely impersonal; he may be a slave and not notice that he is."[318] He does not desire to be a slave but the citizens of many nations have been brainwashed into modern slavery.

Even an imperfect outside system can be endured as long as one has the consolation of the inward joy. This attitude can certainly be accused of escapism, and religions have been labelled the "opiate for the masses", when people have accepted unjust political systems. Nonetheless, religion made life tolerable for poor people through thousands of years.

It is easily noted in history that there were not many alternatives for the poor and the weak. They either made the best out of their conditions of existence – or died. They had no way to overthrow the system, and when they dared, in final desperation, it mostly ended in death and blood-bath. The 'revolts' are many in history, the 'revolutions' are few. The destitute could bear poverty while finding solace in religion. Still, they were perhaps happier than the privileged few better fed and better clothed.

117. Ancient Roots

Just as each individual and each social group needs to cultivate their past, each country must accept that bygone times become part of what is and what will be. Culture must be true to its essence in history, religion and art or be stifled in a material impasse, a risk that we are facing in our day – East and West. Continuity must exist side by side with transformation.

Culture is a comprehensive network of tradition, convention, ritual and practice. One can speak of more other-determined cultures and more inner-determined cultures. The many-faceted culture of India has the emphasis on subjective and spontaneous illumination, whereas modern western traditions turned to scientific discoveries and mechanical inventions. Until the Middle Ages, Europe, too, evinced inwardness

---

[318] W. Herberg 1958, p. 117.

and subjectivity. As in India there were two worlds, the world of sense, and the absolute world, 'veiled' off from the sensory world. In India the balanced view of reality was intact from the early *Upanishads* era (between eighth and fifth centuries B.C.) until this day whereas the West gradually changed and became a single material world.

China, too, manifests a continuous culture. It matches interiority and exteriority and strives for the Mean in things.[319] Contentment and moderation lay at the very heart of this traditional philosophy. These and other virtues were a strait jacket but in fact the ethical cement that glued people and society together.

The Far East, China first and then Korea, Japan, Vietnam and Mongolia formed one civilization that was Confucian, Taoist, Buddhist or Shintoist. In spite of variety they formed a unity with China in the centre. If India and Hinduism are added, we have an eastern sphere which has many components in common. Over this immense stretch of land and people the irrational goes hand in hand with the rational. The question is whether China and the entire East does not present ways of life which are close to ideal. Today Japan seems to have become an outer Mammon culture along western lines and China and India seem heading in the same direction. However, once one scratches the surface, one will detect that the old cultures are still alive, China and Japan more this-worldly and India more other-worldly.

Today we are in the happy position that all cultures form a cohesive mosaic. They can learn from each other. Fundamentalism must be discarded and truth be accepted in different shapes. The intuition and contemplation of eastern cultures should merge with the western intellectual and rational culture, creating an eclectic spiritual civilization for all mankind.

118. The Global View

Until the present day people lived in 'provincial' realities, so it was natural to hold provincial views of the world. As they saw everything locally, they also perceived religion in a narrow, parochial light. Now the globe

[319] As Confucius says, "Perfect is the virtue which is according to the Constant Mean."

has irrevocably become worldwide in scope, and people have begun to think in terms of a single humanity. Borders have become obsolete with modern communications and distances no more. It was natural to regard religion and philosophy on a regional basis when the world was divided in feudal portions which competed with each other. Today, however, when the world has become one entity and is gradually approaching political unity, man is justified in striving towards a heightened awareness of sacred values. Unfortunately the task is not so simple as it seems natural. Learning reaches out across the globe and there is little regional scientific thought. This is plain and obvious. In contrast, religions and religious institutions are conservative and the unity of religious imagination does not shine distinctly even for spirited people.

A common denominator is required to carry out this task of threading all religions like pearls on a string. This string of beads could be the common *scintilla* of the inner light that is inherent in all faiths and beliefs and in life itself. This may sound optimistic, but if all religions acknowledged that they are all built on the same inner consciousness that varies according to human circumstances, people would find themselves on common ground. It would be understood that they are manifestations of the same truth on the ocean of the universal soul.[320] Man's intuition would be the warp and weft of a world-wide ecumenical weave.

This does not concern only religion. A NEW world without the evils of colour, race, class, nationalism and other isms is equally the goal!

119. Quality and the Eternal

Quality is a manifestation of the Eternal in the world. Whatever has quality possesses a streak of the Eternal. Give something quality, and art is produced. See any piece of art which survives centuries, and you know that it possesses something timeless. It walks the line between temporality and eternity and has stood the test of time. This can be sensed in a painting, a book, a composition, a drama, a movie and otherwise. Surely everyone agrees when he sees Mona Lisa that it possess-

---

[320] J. H. Tuckwell 1915, p. 32.

es some special feature that makes it the main attraction of the Louvre in Paris. The true sign of a good book is that it is read generations after it was first published. Most books are shelved within a year of their publication. The same applies to movies. One can enjoy a movie once, but when one enjoys it again a decade later, one knows that it is first-class. Why are most of Chaplin's movies shown again and again? Surely because they have that special quality required to make them last. As Chaplin said himself: "I worked on them." Products of quality are usually worked on hard. Unfortunately, however, this is often not enough. Time is a stern judge. It wipes out rubbish and only the best slips through its sieve. Perhaps this is why we can usually trust what remains from earlier centuries. Only a sharp eye discerns quality; many reviewers should be happy that the general public is so forgetful.

We can differentiate between inner and outer qualities. The latter are measurable whereas the former are not. The physical and temporal world can be measured and weighed and its constituents can be counted and listed and put under some microscope. They are outer qualities, atoms and molecules. The inner qualities are not quantifiable. A tune cannot be analysed as regards parts without losing the quality of its whole. A tightrope walker cannot deliberate his act without losing his balance. He loses it if he thinks consciously of keeping it, says Blondin.

Why does everyone love a winner? In sports the winner receives the laurel and recognition. As for the art of acting, one senses that one actor outshines another. The Japanese use the term *yûgen*, 'Mysterious quality', to express this. When a *Noh* actor has attained *yûgen* excellence, he possesses the absolute perfection that is beyond comprehension. When a Japanese is asked what *yûgen* means, he answers, "*Yûgen* is beauty and elegance." There is no preciser way to express the experience; it must be felt individually by each spectator.

120. Quality and Goodness

Quality and Goodness overlap. Quality displays Goodness, and vice versa. Goodness, however, stretches further. Goodness is the signum of the person who has achieved his mental equanimity. Who is not touched by the good deed? The sign of people who live the inner-directed life is righteous acts – at the right time. True goodness is characterised by spontaneity; it has the personal touch that convinces. Official deeds may have the same effect but do not always show true altruism. Take a glance at the well-meant assistance performed by international organizations to poor nations. The projects are necessary but often lack the grace of empathy and spontaneity. Oftentimes superiority and authority are more visible than humility.

Why does inner goodness move us, even to tears? There must be something in us that relates to such situations, something emotive and tender that generates excitement. This aspect of our life is much exploited in literature, drama and film, and has the same response on every continent, on both men and women. Goodness is also mentioned in all philosophy as the first among the virtues, heavenly or god-given. When the term 'love' is used, usually it is goodness that is referred to. In Greek thought goodness was the first virtue and the compelling force of Creation. In Chinese ideology, *jen*, usually translated as 'goodness' or 'benevolence', is also the highest virtue encompassing all other virtues. It is man's central virtue. Confucius asserts that it is the thread that runs through all and finds expression in rites and ceremonial life. His grandson Tzu-ssu (ca. 481-402 B.C.) says, "Goodness and wisdom (*chih*) are virtues (*te*) inherent in man and are the bridge (*tao*) bringing together the outer and the inner."[321] *Jen* was so much in the midst of the later Neo-Confucian teaching that it was referred to as '*jen* metaphysics'; it is close to the love gospel of the Christian teaching. Courage was also often counted as a Chinese virtue, and wisdom, goodness and courage were considered specific male qualities.

Mencius proved that *jen*, 'goodness', is inborn in man: Anyone witnessing a child about to fall into a well is instinctively terrified and wishes to save it. Altruism comes from the heart, is spontaneous and without calculation. From Mencius' time onwards there were innumerable discussions as to whether human nature was 'good' or 'bad'. According to Mencius man was fundamentally 'good' and to Hsün Tzu man was basically 'bad.' Confucius himself steered a middle course, regarding man as both 'good' and 'bad'. His Golden Rule with its principle of reciprocity said that "What I do not wish others to do to me, I also do not wish to do

---

[321] Translation by E. R. Hughes, quoted in F. S. C. Northrop 1946, p. 329. For Confucius, see *ibid.* pp. 323-328.

to others."[322] In contradiction, Christ said, only more positively: "All what you wish others to do to you, you do to them." This ethical rule is found in all religion and wisdom from their time onwards. Man has the kindness that emanates from his inmost self. Light and dark vie in his nature.

In Greek thought, the true and the beautiful adjoin goodness. Like a clover leaf they display the Eternal in the world. Manifestations of beauty and grace contain truth and goodness. This is just as true East and West. With all three of them one enters the sacred order, and witnesses the blessedness of divine life. Without one of them the clover leaf exhibits neither Eternity nor Heaven. To appreciate the clover leaf, however, requires the wisdom that only self-observation, introspection, poise and inner calm can offer. According to Plato, goodness bestows beauty on the soul, heart and mind and lends richness and meaning to existence.

Hand in hand with goodness goes righteousness. If goodness is the inner side of man, righteousness is the outer. Goodness finds its natural expression in righteous acts. Social norms must reflect both inspiration and rational reflection. In Confucian thinking, *jen*, goodness, and *i*, righteousness, mostly combine with *li*, ritual life, and *chih*, wisdom: outer and inner life in four terms. Inner life comes first, outer life follows.

121. All in the Eyes

The eyes are the centre of a person, his seeing and knowing the world. They are the balancing region of the psyche, not merely of feeling and willing, but also of moral knowing and learning. They can look into the immensity of the galaxies, and into the immeasurable soul. As much as we have extraspective eyes, we have introspective eyes. The mental eyes can penetrate as far into the soul as the physical eyes into the cosmos. The same eyes gaze in both directions. Our happiness demands that we travel inwards to the same extent that we travel outwards.

We must remember that "the light of the body is the eye." Further that "when your eye is sound, your whole body is filled with light; but when it is diseased your body too is all darkness" and that "when thine eye is single, thy body is also full of light, but when "thine eye" is evil, the body

[322] *Lun Yü* XV: 23.

is full of darkness. And that when the faculty of sight is utilised appropriately "thy whole body will have no part dark, and the whole shall be full of light, as when the bright shining of a candle doth give thee light."[323]

Christ indicates a central existential truth often repressed and forgotten in the labyrinth of supernatural concepts when he states that, in order to shine, we must have sound eyes. We shall go through life illuminated by a light shining inwards – and outwards. Thus it is said that "a kind man is recognised by his shining eyes." Shakespeare expressed likewise with much lucidity that all is in the eyes.

By journeying inwards one recognises the existence of the lucid stream of consciousness that is life itself. Just as when one looks into the foliage of a tree and into a blue sky, one pierces into the multicoloured world of the soul. One does not need to close the eyes. Rather to leave the eyes open, and let them roll around and zero in on that central point which sees nothing particular outwards but has its way inwards. As a candle which stands on a clean table casts no shadows, this light shines through the heart obliterating whatever disturbances, transforming darkness into light. The immediacy of feeling lead outwards into the finite world and inwards into the infinite Eternal. "The good and simple and kind have these qualities in their eyes and they are not hidden," says Marcus Aurelius in his *Meditations*.

The technique lies in directing the eyes. The eyes are viewing the essences inwards and the phenomena outwards. Plotinus says that they exist in the middle of the human psyche like a mirror, reflecting the soul inwards and the mind outwards. When correctly directed, they evince the inner truth for you, when misplaced are unably to do so. That they 'see' is not the most essential part; a blind person can experience the same miracle with his 'eyes.' You 'see' also in your dreams and "it is only your heart that sees the truth."

The 'eyes' decide, accordingly, whether one lives conditionally or unconditionally. All life is contingent and dependent upon how circumstances evolve. Once the transcendent function of man has become part of his tapestry of life, there will also be an unconditional component in a decision. In most situations the conditional part is unavoidable. We have the freedom of choice to drive on the right side of the road and

[323] *Luke*, 11: 34-36.

within definite speed limits – and live longer. When it comes to the genuine existential situations, which concern life and death, however, inward light is called for. An important decision requires inner certainty pro or contra. This issue can be incomprehensible for people who do not seek transcendent guidance. For anyone who abides in a living creed, it represents no wonder. It is close to the Taoist's 'action through non-action'. When intuition is permitted partnership in a decision, it often feels as if no decision is taken. When the time is ripe, one moves forth, and everything falls into place. As a Buddhist sutra says: "Use the light within you to revert to your natural clearness of sight. No need to look for it outside."[324]

122. The Goal: Poise and Balance

Inner and outer must exist in harmony. When we feel at one with things, introverted and extraverted at the same time, we are on the border between the eternal and temporal, outside both time and space. We experience the temporal in the eternal and the eternal in the temporal. In its clarity and light one dwells in a non-thinking uncommittedness. It is where the eternal signals the right way to go – at the right time.

The designs of the soul are as full of meaning and significance as the spatio-temporal order of the world of appearances. They are at another level of being, outside our criteria of practical thinking and free from the impediments of the other-directed existence. It seems as if 'contingency' is at work as much as 'necessity'. In the end, however, though inexplicable, they fit into the greater design of a person's cycle of life. Immediate thoughts, timeless visions, opportunities and coincidences spring up and play a part when his mind turns inward and comes to rest. It is his duty to grasp them when the Will presents them! The science of life consists in seizing the chances when Chance brings them. They communicate themselves and one is mysteriously aware of them.

One should strive for "a world-view in which science and religion are partners, not rivals."[325]

---

[324] The *Altar Sutra* quoted in J. C. Cooper 1981, p. 101.
[325] K. R. Miller 1999, p. 219.

123. Illness and Suffering

Illness and suffering are unavoidable parts of man's contract with life. They go together with the final hour and all living and being are affected equally. Plants, animals and man share the same fate and we can only attempt to alleviate it – but in the end accept it. This also concerns old age and growing weakness leading unavoidably to the end. This may seem harsh, not least for those who are troubled the most – those who go through long periods of affliction, who are handicapped and suffer in other ways. It is no real comfort that all Creation coexists under the same fate.

Alas, looking in the mirror, seeing the wrinkles, feeling the arthritis, one becomes aware that there is no way to hold back the clock. Time is also part of Creation. It is no pleasure in becoming aware of added years; with inner time balancing outer time one can confront it more resolutely than by merely living a routine existence.

An animal suffers as much and runs the risk of being eaten and plants deteriorate soon after they have bloomed. All Creation lives under the same Heaven and its inscrutable law and as terrestrial existents we just enjoy the existential moments when we flower momentarily on our way from the Eternal to the Eternal. We can be brave and stoic or take refuge in religion but we must accept the inevitable whether in ill or good health – in the perspective of eternity.

124. Death

At the end, death is as natural as birth at the beginning. Birth and death are the poles of life. Birth is the arrival and death the departure. Death is an inescapable part of existence and should not be ignored or suppressed from consciousness. People confront death every day in the news and otherwise and they should not regard it as just an earthly occurrence but place it in a broad perspective of eternity. It should serve as a remembrance of where everyone ends up. Not just in a grave six feet down or as ashes in an urn in a vault or spread in a memorial churchyard. This is the final goal and the end on the temporal side. Man has the abyss of infinity on both sides of this instant of terrestrial existence. Life is only the coming and going on the great ocean of eternity. As one arrives through the tunnel of birth, one leaves through the tunnel of death. One should not see oneself as beginning in nothing and ending in nothing.

Confronting the final crisis of life, one should rather think of oneself as returning to a rich infinity. One should learn to live mindful of this longer extension. "We die only once – and for such a long time," writes T. S. Eliot (1888-1965). There is no end to death. Rational philosophy is of little help. Religion, rather, comes to one's assistance. One should not see oneself as a candle burning for a short while and then ceasing to exist. One should rather regard life as a bridge to and from infinity – where all existence begins and ends. One should not just be absorbed in a finite physical universe of temporary forms. This has become the life style of many today who see nothing but the cleft and neither of the panoramas that stretch before and after. While engrossed in daily activities, one must always remember that life is always *sub specie aeternitatis*! As Jakob Böhme writes,

> He to whom time is the same as eternity
> And eternity the same as time
> Is free from all contention.[326]

Or as Nicholas of Kues says,

> All temporal succession coincides in one and the same Eternal Now. So there is nothing past or future. ... All is present in everything.

Or as Plotinus says,

> There is all one day,
> Series has no place;
> No yesterday and no tomorrow.[327]

Or as Lao Tzu concludes simply, "All going is returning," or as his follower Chuang Tzu asks matter-of-factly, "If life and death are companions, what have I to be anxious about? All Creation is one!"[328]

For a pessimistic view, on the other hand, one can listen to Schopenhauer who compares life and death to "riding a raft through turbulent rapids, struggling to avoid every shoal and rock, only to reach an escarp-

---

[326] Böhme is quoted in D. Loy 2000, p. 39.
[327] Nicholas of Kues and Plotinus are quoted in D. Loy 2000, p. 41.
[328] *Lao Tzu*, ch. 16, and *Chuang Tzu*, ch. 22.

ment where one is hurled down to eternal nothingness."[329] This is the black view expressed by a modern man who sees a meaningless cessation after a meaningless life that contrasts with the hopeful outlook expressed in earlier ages and traditions.

125. AMEN

It is man's duty to allow his life to run its course in the most authentic way, dictated from within. Balanced, it brings happiness to the individual.

The end is the end. Let us finish with an Amen directed to the Eternal that steers and directs. Let us humbly recognise that all is willed by the Eternal. This concerns each existent thing as much as it does Creation in its totality. From somewhere inside comes the force that directs the celestial spheres and gives each leaf a definite pattern.

Let us sing a song of glory to this Divine Will and enjoy the hilarious exhilaration of the existence that is attuned to the All within the amazing Whole.

[329] *Ibid.* p. 71.

Part II: Oneness in Scriptures East and West

1. *Upanishads* (10th? – 5th? century B.C.)

A.

Though the Infinite One is without colour,
He colours the entire universe;
Though immortal,
He is born, lives and dies.
That One is all that was, is, and will be
Yet He is always the same."

He is the Supreme, Unchanging Absolute

He becomes the fire, the sun,
the wind, the moon;
He becomes the starry heavens,
The vast waters, giving life to all.

He becomes the woman, the man
The youth and the maiden too;
He becomes the old fellow
Tottering on his staff;
He becomes every face
Looking in every direction.

He becomes the blue butterfly,
The green parrot with red eyes;
He becomes lightning, the seasons,
The endless seas.

Without birth or death,
Beyond all time and space,
He is the One from whom
Every world is born.[330]

---

[330] Translation in J. Star 1991, p. 5.

B.

The Lord of all,
The knower of all
The beginning and end of all –
That Self dwells in every human heart. Look out – it's gone.
Look in – it's gone.
It cannot be remembered,5tt
It cannot be forgotten.
It cannot be grasped by any possible means.
It is beyond all limits and bounds.
It is pure oneness
where nothing else can exist.

To know it, you must become it!

It is the final resting place of all activity,
peaceful and unchanging,
the ultimate good,
one without a second.
It is the supreme Self.
It, above all else, should be known.[331]

2. *Bhagavad-Gita* (Song of the Lord), (5th? century B.C.)

Divine manifestations

Lord Krishna:
I am the source of everything,
and all worlds come out of Me;
knowing this, the wise one honours me
in the cave of their hearts.

To those of unswerving devotion
who worship me with love,

---

[331] J. Star 1991, p. 9.

I give the boon of discrimination
by which they come to me.

Dwelling within
as pure consciousness
I destroy the darkness born of ignorance
with the shining lamp og true knowledge.

I am the Supreme Self
dwelling in the hearts of all creatures;
they are born in me, sustained by me,
and in the end, return to me.

Listen Arjuna, I can only tell you of
my most prominent forms;
for my divine power
is endless in extent

Of sun gods, I am Vishnu,
of lights, the radiant sun;
I am chief among the wind gods
the moon in the starry sky.

Among rituals, I am the chanting of sacred names;
among gods, I am Indra, king of Heaven;
among sense organs, I am the mind,
and the pure intelligence of all beings.

I am the glorious Shiva among gods of destruction,
Lord of Wealth among the keepers of fortune;
I am the pure flame among the fire gods,
the great Meru among mountain peaks.

O, Arjuna, know me as instructor of gods,
chief of heavenly priests;
of generals I am Skanda, god of war,
of bodies of water, I am the ocean.
Among great Sages, I am Brighu,

among words, I am the eternal sound OM;
of sacrifices, I am the repetition of God's Name,
of all that is immovable, I am the Himalayas. ...[332]

3. Lao Tzu (ca. 604-531 B.C.), *Tao-Te-Ching* (6th-5th century B.C.)

That which can be called the Tao
  is not the Eternal Tao
That which can be called the Name
  is not the Eternal Name

Tao is both Named and Nameless
As Nameless, it is
  the root of Heaven and Earth
As named, it is
  the Mother of all things

A mind ever free of its own process
  beholds the true miracle of Tao
A mind ever lost in its own process
  sees only the forms of this world

Tao and this world seem different,
  but in truth they are one and the same
The only difference is what we call them.

How deep and mysterious this unity is
  How profound, how great!
It is the truth beyond the truth,
  the mystery beyond the mind
It is the path to all wonder,
  the gate to the ecstatic nature of everything!

(...)

---

[332] J. Star 1991, pp. 10-11.

Look at it and do not see it:
We call it invisible.'
Listen to it and do not hear it:
We call it inaudible.
Touch it and do not feel it:
We call it subtle ...

Infinite and boundless, it cannot be named.
It belongs to the realm of no beings.
It may be called the shape of no-shape,
It may be called the form of no-form.

Vague and obscure!
Meet it, yet you cannot see its head.
Follow it, yet you cannot see its back.[333]

(...)

Something formless, complete in itself
Time before Heaven and Earth
Tranquil, vast, standing alone, unchanging
It provides for all things yet cannot be exhausted
It is the Mother of the Universe
I do not know its name
  so I call it "Tao"
Forced to name it further
I call it
  "Greater than the Greatest"
  "The End of all Endings"
I call it
  "That which is Beyond the Beyond"
  "That to which All Things Return"[334]

(...)

---

[333] From *Tao-Te-Ching*, ch. 1 and ch. 14.
[334] Translation in J. Star 1991, p. 33.

Being and Non-Being produce one another
Hard and easy complete one another,
Long and short are relative to one another
High and low are dependent on one another,
Tones and voice harmonize with one another,
First and last succeed one another.[335]

(...)

Cultivate simplicity
Embrace your original nature
Cut away selfishness
Have few desires[336]

4. Chuang Tzu, *The Inner Law* (4th century B.C.)

He whose law is within himself
Walks in hiddenness
His acts are not influenced
By approval or disapproval.
He whose law is outside himself
Directs his will to what is
Beyond his control
And seeks
To extend his power
Over objects

He who walks in hiddenness
Has light to guide him
In all his acts
He who seeks to extend his control
Is nothing but an operator.
While he thinks he is

[335] F. C. Happold 1963, p. 152.
[336] S. H. Ruppenthal 2004, p. 36.

Surpassing others,
Others see him merely
Straining, stretching,
To stand on tiptoe.

When he tries to extend his power
Over objects,
Those objects gain control
of him.

He who is controlled by objects
loses possession of his self:
If he no longer values himself,
How can he value others?
If he no longer value others,
He is abandoned.
He has nothing left!

There is no deadlier weapon than the will!
The sharpest sword
Is not equal to it!
There is no robber so dangerous
As Nature (*Yang* and *Yin*).
Yet it is not nature
That does the damage:
It is man's own will! [337]

Chuang Tzu (Great Knowledge)

Great knowledge sees all in one.
Small knowledge breaks down into the many.

When the body sleeps, the soul is enfolded in One.
When the body wakes, the openings begin to function.

---

[337] T. Merton 1965, pp. 136-137.

They resound with every encounter
With all varied business of life, the strivings of the heart;
Men are blocked, perplexed, lost in doubt.
Little fears eat away their peace of heart.
Great fears swallow them whole.
Arrows shoot at a target: hit and miss, right and wrong.
That is what men call judgment, decision.
Their pronouncements are as final
as treatises between emperors.
O, they make their point!
Yet their arguments fall faster and feabler
Than dead leaves in autumn and winter.
Their talks flow out like piss,
never to be recovered.
They stand at last, blocked, bound and gagged,
Choked up like old drain pipes.
The mind fails. It shall not see light again.

Pleasure and rage
Sadness and joy
Hopes and regrets
Change and stability
Weakness and decision
Impatience and sloth:
All are sounds from the same flute,
All mushrooms from the same wet mould.
Day and night follow one another and come upon us
Without our seeing how they sprout.

If there were no "that"
There would be no "this."
If there were no "this"
There would be nothing for all these winds to play on.
So far can we go.
But how shall we understand
What brings it about?

One may well suppose the True Governor
To be behind it all. That such a Power works
I can believe. I cannot see his form.[338]

5. Chu Hsi (1130-1200), *Reflections on Things at Hand*

The essence of *Tao* is an all-encompassing wholeness, which contains everything and is such of itself. There cannot be even the fineness of a hair in differentiating the fine and the coarse, the root and tip, the secondary and the primary. No matter how meticulous, orderly, detailed or precise, nothing will ever harm its wholeness.

6. From the *Lotus Sutra* (4th century)

I look upon all things
as being universally equal
I have no mind to favour this nor that,
to love one or hate another.
I am without greed or attachment
and without limitation or hindrance.
At all times, for all things
I preach the Law equally,
as I would for a single person
I bring fullness and satisfaction ...

Pursue not the outer entanglements,
Dwell not in the Inner Void;
Be serene in the oneness of things,
And dualism vanishes by itself.
As long as you tarry in dualism
How can you realize oneness?
The two exist because of the One,
But hold not even to this One;

---

[338] T. Merton 1965, pp. 40-41.

When a mind is not dIsturbed,
The ten thousand things offer no offence.
One in All,
All in One –
If only this were realized,
No more worry about your not being perfect.[339]

7. Seneca (ca. 2 B.C. – 65 A.D.)

What is God? –
The Mind of the universe.
what is He? –
All that you see, and all that you don't see

Guide and guardian of the universe;
Soul and spirit of the world;
Builder and master of so great a work –
to Him all names belong.
Would you call Him Destiny?
You will not err:
Cause of causes, on Him all depends.
Had you rather say Providence?
This will be all rIght:
By His plan the world is watched over
insuring that it goes safely through its motions
Or Nature?
This title does him no wrong:
Of Him all things are born, and in him all things live.
Or UnIverse?
You are nor mistaken:
He is all that we see,
wholly present in every part,
sustaining this entire Creation.[340]

---

[339] *The Lotus Sutra*, translation in B. Watson 1968, p. 103.
[340] J. Star 1991, p. 113.

8. Marcus Aurelius (121-180)

Remember that it is the Hidden Power within us that pulls the strings; there lies the guiding force, there is the life, there, one might say, is the man himself. Never think of yourself as a mere body with its various appendages. The body is like the axe of a carpenter: dare we think the axe to be the carpenter himself? Without this Inner Cause, which dictates both action and inaction, the body is of no more use than the weaver's shuttle without a weaver, the writer's pen without a writer, or the coachman's whip without a horse and carriage.[341]

Honour the highest thing in the Universe; it is the power on which all things depend; it is the light by which all of life is guided. Honour the highest within yourself; for it too is the power on which all things depend, and the light by which all life is guided.

DIG WITHIN. Within is the wellspring of Good; and it is always ready to bubble up, IF YOU JUST DIG! ... Waste no more time about great souls and how they should be. Become one yourself! (Emphasis added)[342]

9. St. Augustine (354-430), *Meditationes*

Recognise in yourself something within, within yourself. Leave aside the external things (*relinque foris et vestem tuam et carnem tuam*); descend into yourself; go to that hidden apartment, your soul! If you are far from your own self, how can you draw near to God? Not in the body, but in the mind was man made in the image of God. In his likeness let us seek God; in his own image recognise the Creator.

10. Jalaluddin Rumi (Sufi religion, 1207-1273)

I know nothing of two worlds
  all I know is the One
I seek only One,
I know only One,

[341] Marcus Aurelius, *Meditations*, 10: 38.
[342] *Ibid.* pp. 106-107.

I find only One
  and I sing of only One.
I am so drunk with the wine of the Beloved
  that both worlds have slipped from my reach.
Now I have no business here,
  Save to reach for the cup of my Beloved.[343]

Flowers every night
blossom in the sky;
Peace in the Infinite;
At peace am I.

11. Meister Eckhart (1260-1328)

(1) We ought to understand God equally in all things
  for God is equally in all things.
All beings love one another
All creatures are interdependent.

(2) The seed of God is in all of us
  Now
  the seed of a pear tree
  grows into a pear tree
  and a hazel seed
  grows into a hazel tree
a seed of God
  grows into
  God.

(3) This I know.
That the only way to live
  is like the rose
which lives
  without a why.

---

[343] Marcus Aurelius, *Meditations*, p. 123.

(4) What is life?
Life is a kind of boiling over
in which a thing wells up within itself,
floods itself and overflows
pouring itself into all of its parts
until finally
it spills over
boiling and overflowing
into something eternal as well.

(5) My soul is as young as the day it was created
Yes, and much younger!
In fact, I am younger today than I was yesterday,
and if I am not younger tomorrow than I am today,
I would be ashamed of myself.
People who dwell in God dwell in the eternal now.
There, people can never grow old.
There, everything is present and everything is new.

(6) There
where clinging to things ends
is where God begins to be.
If a cask is to contain wine,
you must first pour out the water
the cask must be bare and empty
Therefore,
if you wish to receive divine joy and God
first pour our your clinging to things.
Everything that is to receive
must and ought to be
empty.
It is a delusion to think
that we can obtain more of God
by contemplation
or by pious devotions
or by religious retreats

than
  by being at the fireplace
  or by working in the stable.

Spiritually
is not to be learned
by flight from the world,
by turning away from things,
or by turning solitary and going apart from the world.
Rather,
we must learn an inner solitude
wherever or with whomsoever we may be.
We must learn to penetrate things
and find things there.

God's ground is my ground
and my ground is God's ground.
Here I live on my own
as God lives on his own.
All our works
should work out of this most ground
without a why or a wherefore.
Then,
God and the soul
do one work together
eternally
and very fruitfully.
Then,
all that this person works
God works.
And just as I can do almost nothing without God'
so too God can accomplish nothing
apart from me.[344]

[344] M. Fox 1983, pp. 26-93.

12. John Ruysbroeck (1294-1381)

The grace of God ... is an inward thrust and urge of the Holy Ghost, driving forward our spirit from within and exciting it toward all virtues. This grace flows from within, and not from without. ... His inward thrust or working within us, be it natural or supernatural, is nearer to us and more intimate to us, than our own working is. ... God works in us from within outwards, but all creatures work from outwards inwards. ... Thus all the gifts of God, and the voice of God, come from within, in the unity of our spirit, and not from without. ... Knowledge of ourselves teaches us whence we come, where we are and whither we are going...[345]

13. Blaise Pascal (1632-1662)

I see nothing but infinities on all sides, enclosing me like an atom, or a shadow which lasts only for a moment and does not return. All I know is that I must shortly die but what I know least about is death itself, which I cannot avoid. In the same way that I do not know where I came from, neither do I know where I am going. ...

> God of Abraham, God of Isaac, God of Jacob,
> Not the God of philosophers and scholars.
> Absolute Certainty: Beyond reason. Joy. Peace.
> Forgetfulness of the world and everything but God.
> The world has not known thee, but I have known thee.
> Joy! joy! joy! tears of joy![346]

14. Baruch Spinoza (1632-1677)

[The *human* mind] *teaches* us that we share in the divine nature, and that we share the more, the more perfect our actions are, and the more we understand God. This doctrine, therefore, besides giving us true peace of mind, also teaches us where our greatest happiness or blessedness lies: in the knowledge of God, by which we are led to do only those things

[345] Quotation in F. C. Happold 1963, p. 285, and in J. C. Cooper 1981, p. 87.
[346] B. Pascal 1995, p. 178,

that love and piety advise. From this we clearly understand how far astray from the true estimation of virtue are those who expect to be honoured by God with the greatest rewards for their virtue and good deeds, – as if virtue and the service of God were not happiness itself.[347]

15. Thomas Traherne (1637?-1674)

You never enjoy the world aright, till the sea itself floweth in your veins, till you are clothed with the heavens, and crowned with the stars; and perceive yourself to be the sole heir of the whole world, and more than so, because men are in it who are every one sole heirs as well as you. Till you can sing and rejoice and delight in God, as misers do in gold, and kings in sceptres, you never enjoy the world.[348]

16. Swami Muktananda (1908-1982)

God dwells as fully in you as in the highest heavens. ... The universe within is superior to that without. ... Sages have spent their whole lives trying to behold the scintillating divine spark that lies within the heart. ... O soul of man! What joy could beckon you in the external world while such an infinite treasure of marvels lies within? ... As the magnificent radiance sparkles in meditation, ... you will see the whole world as radiant. ... Sweet, divine music will ring in your ears. ... and you will be transported with immense delight. ... Your world will quiver with beauty, joy and love. ... Do not give up your worldly life, ... rushing around in search of God in the four directions. ... God belongs to you all. If you call Him with love, ... He will reveal Himself to you. He will grant a vision of the divine light of His love. Then you will know what that you are an embodiment of bliss. ...[349]

---

[347] B. Spinoza 1922, book 2, quotation from S. Mitchell 1991, p. 147.
[348] T. Traherne 1932, p. 2.
[349] J. Star 1991, pp. 226-228.

References

Adams, Douglas, *The Hitchhiker's Guide to Galaxy*, London, 1979.

Allen, R. T., *The Political Thought of F. A. Hayek & Michael Polanyi, Beyond Liberalism*, London, 1998.

Armstrong, Karen, *A History of God*, London, 1993.

——, *A Short History of Myth*, London, 2005a.

——, *God Alert*, in *Utne*, March-April, 2005b.

——, *The Great Transformation*, New York, 2006.

Bahr, Earhard, *Was ist Aufklärung?*, Stuttgart, 1974.

Baillie, John, *Our Knowledge of God*, London, 1939.

Baker, Herschel, *The Wars of Truth*, Harvard, 1952.

Barrett, William, *Irrational Man, A Study of Existential Philosophy*, New York, 1962.

—— (ed.), *Zen Buddhism, Selected Writings of D. T. Suzuki*, New York, 1956.

Bellow, Saul, *Mr. Sammler's Spell*, New York, 1970.

Berdyaev, Nikolai, *The Fate of Man in the Modern World*, Ann Arbor, 1961.

Bergson, Henri, *Les deux sources de la morale et de la religion*, English trans. by R. Ashley Audra and Cloudesley Brereton, *The Two Sources of Morality and Religion*, New York, 1935.

——, *L'être et le Néant*, Paris, 1929a.

——, *L'intuition philosophique*, Paris, 1929b.

Berlin, Isaiah, *The Sense of Reality, Studies in Ideas and their History*, London, 1996.

Berlinski, Claire, *Menace in Europe with the Continents Crisis is America's, Too*, New York, 2006.

Blake, William, *The Works of William Blake*, ed. Wordsworth Poetry Library, Hertfordshire, 1995.

Brown, Robert F., *The Later Philosophy of Schelling, The Influence of Böhme on the Works of 1809-1815*, London, 1977.

Bruce, J. Percy, *Chu Hsi and His Masters*, London, 1923.

Calder, Nigel, *The Mind of Man*, London, 1970.

Carrette, Jeremy (ed.), *William James and the Varieties of Religious Experience*, London, 2005.

Carter, Robert E., *Encounter with Enlightenment, A Study of Japanese Ethics*, New York, 2001.

Cassirer, Ernst, *An Essay on Man*, Yale University Press, 1944.

Chaigne, Louis, *Paul Claudel, The Man and the Mystic*, New York, 1961. Original: *Vie de Paul Claudel.*

Chardin, Teilhard de, *The Phenomenon of Man*, Paris, 1955.

Chuang Chun-chieh, *"Time" and "Supertime" in Chinese Historical Thinking*, in Chuang C.-c. and J. B. Henderson (ed.), *Notions of Time*, pp. 19-41.

Chuang Chun-chieh and Henderson, John B. (ed.), *Notions of Time*, Hong Kong, 2006.

Coakley, Sarah, *Christ Without Absolutes, A Study of the Christology of Ernst Troeltsch*, Oxford, 1988.

Cohen, L. Jonathan, *The Principles of World Citizenship*, Oxford, 1954.

Cohen, Sidney, *The Beyond Within*, New York, 1964.

Comte-Sponville, André, *Petit traité des grandes vertus*, Paris, 1995.

Conrad, Joseph, *An Outpost of Progress*, London, 1898.

——, *Chance*, London, 1913.

——, *Heart of Darkness*, London, 1902.

——, *Karain. A Memory*, in *Tales of Unrest*, pp. 11-29, Leipzig, 1898 (Tauchnitz Edition, vol. 3300).

——, *Tales of Unrest*, Leipzig, 1898.

——, *The Mirror of the Sea*, London, 1906, Swedish translation, *Havets spegel*, Skara, 1966.

Cooper, Jean C., *Yin & Yang, The Taoist Harmony of Opposites*, Wellingborough, 1981.

Cornford, Francis M., *From Religion to Philosophy, A Study in the Origins of Western Speculation*, New York, 1957.

Cox, Harvey, *Turning East*, New York, 1977.

Creel, Herrlee G., *Chinese Thought From Confucius To Mao tse-tung*, Chicago, 1953.

——, *Sinism: A Study of the Evolution of the Chinese World-view*. London, 1929.

Da Liu, *The TAO and Chinese Culture*, New York, 1979.

Damasio, Antonio R., *Descartes' Error: Emotion, Reason and the Human Brain*, Oxford, 1996.

——, *Looking for Spinoza, Joy, Sorrow and the Feeling Brain*, Orlando, 2003.

Danto, Arthur C., *Mysticism and Morality, Oriental Thought and Moral Philosophy*, New York and London, 1972.

Dennet, Daniel C., *Breaking the Spell, Religion as a Natural Phenomenon*, London, 2006.

Dickens, Robert, *Thoreau: The Complete Individualist*, New York, 1974.

Durant, Will, *The Story of Philosophy*, New York, 1953.

Durant, Will and Ariel, *Rousseau and Revolution*, New York, 1967.

Duyvendak, Jan J. L., *Hsün-tzu on the Rectification of Names*, T'oung Pao, XXIII, Leiden, 1924.

Eccles, John C., *Evolution of the Brain: Creation of the Self*, London, 1989.

——, *The Human Psyche*, Berlin, 1980.

Eccles, John C. and Robinson, Daniel N., *The Wonder of Being Human, Our Brain and our Mind*, London, 1984.

Einhorn, Lena, *Vad hände på vägen till Damascus*, Stockholm, 2006.

Einhorn, Stefan, *En dold Gud*, Stockholm, 1998.

——, *Konsten att vara snäll*, Stockholm, 2005.

Einstein, Albert, *Mein Weltbild*, Amsterdam, 1934.

Ekman, Paul, *Emotions Revealed*, New York, 2003.

Eliot, Charles, *Hinduism and Buddhism, an Historical Sketch*, 3 vols. London, 1921.

Eliot, T. S., *Burnt Norton*, London, 1941.

Eysenck, Hans J., *Uses and Abuses of Psychology*, Penguin Book, London, 1952.

Firchov, Peter Edgerly, *Reluctant Modernists: Aldous Huxley and Some Contemporaries, A Collection of Essays*, London, 2002.

Fischer, Kevin, *Converse in the Spirit, William Blake, Jakob Böhme, and the Creative Spirit*, Cranbury, 2004.

Flynn-Hui, Kathleen, *Beyond the Blonde*, New York, 2005.

Fordham, Frieda, *An Introduction to Jung's Psychology*, London, 1953.

Fox, Adam, *Dean Inge*, London, 1960.

Fox, Matthew, *Meditations with Meister Eckhart*, Rochester, Vermont, 1983.

Gaarder, Jostein, *Sophie's World*, Oslo, 1991 (New York, 1994).

Geldsetzer, Lutz and Hong, Han-ding, *Grundlagen der chinesischen Philosophie*, Stuttgart, 1998.

Gerson, Lloyd P., *Plotinus*, London and New York, 1994.

Gilson, Étienne, *A Gilson Reader, Selections from the Writings of Etienne Gilson*, ed. Anton C. Pegis, New York, 1957.

——, *God and Philosophy*, Yale, 1941.

Gleick, James, *Sir Isaac Newton*, New York, 2004.

Goethes Werke, ed. Gerhart Hauptmann, Berlin, no date.

Goethe's Werke, ed. Uwe Lassen, Hamburg, no date.

Graham, Dom Aelred, *The End of Religion, Autobiographical Explorations*, New York and London, 1971.

Gundry, Mark, *Beyond Psyche, Symbol and Transcendence in C. G. Jung*, New York, 2006.

Haldane, Viscount Richard B., *Autobiography*, 1929.

Happold, F. C., *Mysticism, A Study and an Anthology*, London, 1963.

Hardin, Garrett, *Nature and Man's Fate*, New York, 1958.

Hawton, Hector, *Philosophy for Pleasure*, New York, 1956.

Hayward, John, *The Penguin Book of English Verse*, New York, 1956.

Hedenius, Ingemar, *Livets mening*, Stockholm, 1964.

Heisenberg, Werner, *Across the Frontiers*, New York, 1974.

——, *Das Naturbild der heutigen Physik*, Hamburg, 1955.

——, *Physics and Beyond, Encounters and Conversations*, London, 1971.

——, *Physics and Philosophy, The Revolution in Modern Science*, London, 1959.

Herberg, Will, *Four Existentialist Theologians*, New York, 1958.

Herneck, Friedrich, *Albert Einstein, Ein Leben für Wahrheit, Menschlichkeit und Frieden*, Berlin, 1963.

——, *Einstein und sein Weltbild*, Berlin, 1976.

Hick, John, *Biology and the Soul*, Cambridge, 1972.

——, *Death and Eternal Life*, London, 1976.

Hofmannsthal, Hugo von, *Libretto for Richard Strauss' Der Rosenkavalier*, 1911.

Horgan, John, *The Undiscovered Mind*, London, 1999.

Howarth, Herbert, *The Tiger's Heart, Eight Essays on Shakespeare*, London, 1970.

Hu Shih, *The Chinese Renaissance*, Chicago, 1934.

Hughes, Ernest R., *Chinese Philosophy in Classical Times*, New York, 1942.

Hughes, Glenn, *The Politics of the Soul*, New York, 1999.

Hume, David, *A Treatise of Human Nature* (1738), ed. L. A. Selby-Bigge, Oxford, 1988.

Huxley, Julian, *Knowledge, Morality, & Destiny*, New York, 1957; original title: *New Bottles for New Wine*.

Inge, William R., *Conclusion*, in J. Needham, *Science Religion and Reality*, pp. 347-389, New York, 1925.

——, *Mysticism in Religion*, Chicago, 1948.

Jacobson, Mogens Chrom, *David Hume, Politik og æstetik. Udvalgte essays*, Frederiksberg, 2000.

James, William, *The Varieties of Religious Experience, A Study in Human Nature*, New York, 1963.

Jaspers, Karl, *Way to Wisdom, An Introduction to Philosophy*, New Haven, 1954.

Johansson, Frans, *The Medici Effect, Breakthrough Insights at the Intersection of Ideas, Concepts and Cultures*, Harvard, 2004.

Jones, E. Stanley, *Mahatma Gandhi*, Stockholm, 1949.

Jung, Carl Gustav, *Jung on the East*, ed. J. J. Clarke, London, 1995.

——, *Modern Man in Search of a Soul*, London, 1984.

Jung, Carl Gustav and Wilhelm, Richard, *The Secret of the Golden Flower*, London, 1962.

——, *The Undiscovered Self*, New York, 1957.

Kierkegaard, Søren, *Øieblikket*, Copenhagen, 1854.

Klein, Naomi, *The Shock Doctrine*, London, 2007.

Klein, Stefan, *Alles Zufall*, Hamburg, 2004.

Kochanek, Hermann (ed.), *Die Botschaft der Mystik*, München, 1998.

Koestler, Arthur, *The Ghost in the Machine*, Pan Books, 1971.

——, *The Lotus and the Robot*, New York, 1960.

Kohn, Livia, *Early Chinese Mysticism, Philosophy and Soteriology in the Taoist Tradition*, Princetgon, 1992.

Krutch, Joseph Wood, *The Measure of Man*, New York, 1953.

Lack, David, *Evolutionary Theory and Christian Belief. The Unresolved Conflict*, London, 1961.

Langer, Susanne K., *Philosophy in a New Key, A study in the Symbolism of Reason, Rite and Art*, Harvard, 1956.

Läpple, Alfred, *Ketzer und Mystiker*, München, 1988.

Lasch, Christopher, *The Revolt of the Elites – and the Betrayal of Democracy*, New York, 1995.

——, *The True and Only Heaven, Progress and Its Critics*, New York and London, 1991.

Lau, D. C., *Confucius' The Analects (Lun Yü)*, Hong Kong, 1983.

Leakey, Richard E., *The Making of Mankind*, London, 1981.

Legge, James, *The Four Books*, Hong Kong, 1861-1872.

Le Guin, Ursula K., *Lao Tzu: Tao-Te-Ching*, Boston and London, 1997.

Lewis, Clive Staples, *The Four Loves*, London, 1960.

Lidin, Olof G., *From Taoism to Einstein*, London, 2006.

Lind, Lis, *Søren Kierkegaard själv*, Stockholm, 2000.

Lovejoy, Arthur O., *The Revolt Against Dualism*, London, 1960.

Lovell, Bernard, *Das unendliched Weltall, Geschichte der Kosmologie von der Antike bis zur Gegenwart*, C. H. Beck, München, 1981.

Loy, David, *Lack and Transcendence, The Problem of Death and Life in Psychotherapy, Existentialism, and Buddhism*, New York, 2000.

MacIntyre, Alasdair, *A Short History of Ethics*, New York, 1966.

MacNeice, Louis, *Goethe's Faust, abridged version and translation,* Oxford, 1972.

Magee, Bryan, *The Story of Philosophy*, London, 1998.

Mainzer, Klaus, *ZEIT, Von der Urzeit zur Computerzeit*, München, 2002.

Malinowski, Bronislaw, *Magic, Science and Religion*, New York, 1948

Marcus Aurelius, *Meditations*, Oxford, 1989.

Martin, Edwin T., *Thomas Jefferson: Scientist*, New York, 1952.

McLeod, Hugh, *Secularisation in Western Europe 1848-1914*, London, 2000.

Merton, Thomas, *The Way of Chuang Tzu*, New York, 1965.

Metzger, Charles R., *Thoreau and Whitman, A Study of Their Esthetics*, Seattle, 1961.

Metzger, Thomas A., *Escape from Predicament, Neo-Confucianism and China's Evolving Political Culture*, New York, 1977.

Miller, Kenneth R., *Finding Darwin's God, A Scientist's Search for Common Ground Between God and Evolution*, New York, 1999.

Milosz, Czeslaw, *Själar i fångenskap*, Stockholm, 1996; Polish original: *Zniewolony umysl.*

Mindell, Arnold, *River's Way, The Process Science and Dreambody*, London, 1985.

Mishima Yukio, *Confessions of a Mask*, London, 1958.

——, *The Temple of Dawn*, New York, 1973.

Mitchell, Stephen (ed.), *The Enlightened Mind, An Anthology of Sacred Prose*, New York, 1991.

Moberg, Åsa, *Efteråt*, Smedjebacken, 2002.

Munro, Donald J., *The Concept of Man in Early China*, Stanford, 1969.

Nagy, Marilyn, *Philosophical Issues in the Psychology of C. G. Jung*, New York, 1991.

Nathanson, Tenney, *Whitman's Presence, Body, Voice, and Writing in Leaves of Grass*, New York, 1992.

Niebuhr, Reinhold, *An Interpretation of Christian Life*, London, 1948.

——, *The Children of Light and the Children of Darkness*, New Haven, 1944.

Nieuwenhove, Rik van, *Jan van Ruusbroec, Mystical Theologian of the Trinity*, Notre Dame, 2003.

Northrop, F. S. C., *The Meeting of East and West*, Yale, 1946.

Parkes, Henry Bamford, *The Divine Order, Western Culture in the Middle Ages & the Renaissance*, London, 1970.

Pascal, Blaise, *Les Pensées*, first published 1670 as *Pensées sur la religion et quelques autres sujets*, translated by H. Levy, *Blaise Pascal Pensées and Other Writings*, New York, 1995.

Patka, Frederick, *Existentialist Thinkers & Thought*, New York, 1962.

Pirsig, Robert M., *Zen and the Art of Motocycle Maintenance*, New York, 1974.

Planck, Max, *Wege zur physikalischen Erkenntnis*, Leipzig, 1944.

Polanyi, Michael, *Personal Knowledge*, Chicago, 1958.

—— (ed.), *Society, Economics & Philosophy, Selected Papers*, London, 1997.

——, *The Study of Man*, Chicago, 1959.

Popper, Karl R. and Eccles, John C., *The Self and Its Brain*, London, 1977.

Post, Laurens van der, *Flamingo Feather, Story of Africa*, London, 1965.

——, *Journey into Russia*, London, 1964.

——, *Jung and the Story of our Time*, London, 1976 (Penguin Books, 1978).

——, *Venture to the Interior*, London, 1952.

——, *Yet Being Someone Other*, London, 1982

Rawlinson, Nick, *William Blake's Comic Vision*, New York, 2003.

Reinhardt, Kurt F., *The Existentialist Revolt*, New York, 1952.

Ricard, Matthieu, *Happiness*, New York, 2006.

Rieff, Philip, *The Feeling Intellect*, Chicago, 1999.

Riesman, David; Glazer, Nathan; Denney, Reuel, *The Lonely Crowd, A Study of the Changing American Character* (abridged), New York, 1953.

Rist, John M., *Plotinus: The Road to Reality*, Cambridge, 1967.

Ross, N. Wilson, *Three Ways of Asian Wisdom: Hinduism, Buddhism, Zen and Their Significance*, London, 1966.

Roth, Harold D., *Psychology and Self-Cultivation in Early Taoistic Thought*, HJAS, vol. 51: 2 (1991), pp. 599-650.

Rougemont, Denis de, *Love in the Western World*, New York, 1956.

Ruppenthal, Stephen H., *The Path of Direct Awakening*, Berkeley, 2004.

Rusk, Ralph L., *The Life of Ralph Waldo Emerson*, New York, 1949.

Schreyer, Lothar, *Deutsche Mystik*, Berlin, ca. 1920.

Shakespeare, William, *The Works of William Shakespeare*, New York, 1937.

Shaw, Bernard, *Heartbreak House*, London, 1919.

Sheen, Fulton J., *Peace of Soul*, New York, 1951.

——, *Way to Happiness*, New York, 1953.

Siu, Ralph G. H., *The Tao of Science. An Essay on Western Knowledge and Eastern Wisdom*, Massachusettes, 1957.

Smith, Thomas V. and Lindeman, Eduard C., *The Democratic Way of Life*, New York, 1951.

Sorell, Tom, *Descartes Reinvented*, New York, 2005.

Sowell, Thomas, *The Quest for Cosmic Justice*, New York, 1999.

Sparks, J. Gary, *At the Heart of Matter, Synchronicity and Jung's Spiritual Testament*, Toronto, 2007.

Spinoza, Baruch, *Ethics* (1677), tr. Stockholm, 1922.

Star, Jonathan, *Two Suns Rising, A Collection of Sacred Writings*, New York, 1991.

Stark, Rodney, *For the Glory of God: How Monotheism Led to Reformations, Science, Witch-hunts, and the End of Slavery*, Princeton, 2003.

——, *The Rise of Christianity*, Princeton, 1996.

——, *The Victory of Reason*, New York, 2005.

Stein, Murray, *Jung's Map of the Soul*, Chicago, 1998.

Strawson, Peter F., *Analysis and Metaphysics, An Introduction to Philosophy*, Oxford, 1992.

Taylor, Eugene, *Metaphysics and Consciousness in James's Varieties*, in Carrette, Jeremy R. (ed.), *William James and the Varieties of Religious Experience*, pp. 11-26.

Taylor, Rodney L., *The Confucian Way of Contemplation, Okada Takehiko and the Tradition of Quiet-Sitting*, Columbia, South Carolina, 1988.

The Oxford Dictionary of Quotations, Oxford, 1966.

Thoreau, Henry David, *Walden*, New York, 1949.

Thorpe, William Homan, *Animal Nature and Human Nature*, London, 1974.

——, *Biology, Psychology and Belief*, Cambridge, 1961.

——, *Purpose in the World of Chance*, Oxford, 1978.

Torrance, Robert H., *The Spiritual Quest, Transcendence in Myth, Religion, and Science*, Berkeley, 1994.

Toynbee, Arnold J., *East to West, A Journey Round the World*, London, 1958.

Traherne, Thomas, *Centuries of Meditations*, ed. B. Dobell, London, 1932.

Tuckwell, James Henry, *Religion and Reality, A Study of the Philosophy of Mysticism*, London, 1915.

Vartanian, Aram, *La Mettrie's L'homme Machine, A Study in the Origins of an Idea*, Princeton, 1960.

Waley, Arthur, *The Analects of Confucius, translated and annotated*, London, 1938.

Walsh, William H., *Metaphysics*, New York, 1963.

Ware, James R., *The Sayings of Chuang Tzu*, New York, 1963.

Watson, Burton, *The Complete Works of Chuang Tzu*, New York, 1968.

Watts, Alan W., *Tao, the Watercourse Way*, New York, 1975.

——, *The Supreme Identity*, New York, 1972.

Whitehead, Alfred North, *Science and the Modern World*, Cambridge, 1925.

Whitman, Walt, *Leaves of Grass*, original 1855, Penguin Book, 1959.

Whyte, Lancelot Law, *The Unconscious before Freud*, London, 1979.

Wilder Foote, Henry, *The Religion of an Inquiring Mind*, Boston, 1955.

Wildiers, Norbert M., *An Introduction to Teilhard de Chardin*, New York, 1968.

Wilson, Colin, *Introduction to the New Existentialism*, London, 1966.

Wilson, Edward O., *On Human Nature*, London, 1978.

Wright, Georg Henrik von, *The Varieties of Goodness*, New York, 1963.

Yukawa, Hideki, *Creativity and Intuition, A Physicist looks at East and West*, New York, 1973.

Zaehner, Robert Charles, *Mystik, Harmonie und Dissonanz*, Olten, 1980. Original in English, *Concordant Discord. The Interdependence of Faiths*, Oxford, 1970.

——, *The Living Encyclopedia of Living Faiths*, London, 1971.

Register